n783

MW01517152

MANAGEMENT CONSULTING:

THEORY AND TOOLS FOR SMALL BUSINESS INTERVENTIONS

STEPHEN J. PORTH
St. Joseph's University

MICHAEL SALTIS

1998

DAME
PUBLICATIONS, INC.

Cover Design: Amanda S. Austin

Cover Photo: © **Corel Professional Photos.** Images may have
                     been combined and/or modified to produce final
                     cover art.

© **DAME PUBLICATIONS, INC.—1998**
  7800 Bissonnet—Suite 415
  Houston, TX 77074
  713/995-1000
  713/995-9637—FAX
  800/364-9757
  E-mail: dame.publications@worldnet.att.net
  Website: http://www.damepub.com

All rights reserved. No part of this publication may be reproduced,
stored in a retrieval system, or transmitted, in any form or by any
means, electronic, mechanical, photocopying, recording, or otherwise,
without the prior written permission of the publisher.

ISBN 0-87393-737-6

Library of Congress Card No. 97-77457

Printed in the United States of America.

Dedicated to:

Mary, Stephen, Molly, Leo and Tommy, my wife and children.
With Love and Thanks.   S. P.

My children, Michael, Catherine, Mark, and Caedon, and my wife, Dorrie.
You are a source of Love and Joy.   M. S.

PREFACE

To our knowledge (and we have searched far and wide), there is no extensive, single source of information on the topic of management consulting to *small businesses*. True, volumes of research and writing have been done on management consulting, but very little of it with small businesses in mind. In this sense, our book is the first of its kind. It specifically describes the special, unique aspects of small business interventions, and offers practical advice for managing them.

We have designed and written this book with two distinct, but in many ways related, audiences in mind. First and foremost, it is written for the practicing consultant. Research and specialized knowledge of small business consulting are scarce at a time when both the size and economic impact of the small business sector is growing, and the demand for consulting services flourishes. This book is designed to help consultants understand the needs of small businesses, and to succeed in their small business interventions. Practical, experience–based strategies and tools are described for use in the field.

In addition, we have written the book for those who want to learn more about management consulting, especially students. This book may be used as a resource in management consulting, project management, and other experiential business courses. These types of courses, where students manage a project and interact with a "live organization/client", are part of a growth market on college campuses, as more business schools respond to the call to make their curricula real and practical. It is specifically with our own students in mind that we write this book.

The book is presented in two parts. Part I, comprised of Chapters 1, 2 and 3, describes the background and context of consulting to small businesses. Part II (Chapters 4 through 8 and the two appendices) focuses on the special needs of the small business client, and describes frameworks and tools for successful interventions.

ACKNOWLEDGEMENTS

We are grateful to many people for helping to make this book "happen". Thanks to Pat Weaver, Dan Ingersoll, MaryAnne Badala, Will May, Debbie Berry, and Erin Hungarter for their research contributions. Thanks to our colleagues at St. Joseph's University, for their encouragement of this project, and their ongoing friendship. Thanks to Bernice Brogan and Mary Finelli for administrative assistance. Most of all, we appreciate the patience, love and support of our families, to whom this book is dedicated.

About The Authors

Stephen Porth is Associate Professor of Management at St. Joseph's University in Philadelphia where he teaches, among other courses, Management Consulting at both the executive MBA and undergraduate levels. He has been a consultant to organizations of all sizes, from Fortune 500 companies to nonprofit community-based social agencies. He is a member of the Managerial Consultation Division of the Academy of Management.

Michael Saltis is an entrepreneur, small business owner, and consultant. He recently left Scott Paper Company after a management career of more than 25 years. Mike is also working on a doctoral degree at Temple University and is an adjunct professor at St. Joseph's University, where he teaches management consulting.

TABLE OF CONTENTS

PART I:

The Context of Small Business Consulting

Part 1 examines the background and context of management consulting to small businesses. The unique aspects and subtle nuances of small business consulting are identified and described, and related special client needs are established. A model or framework of small business consulting is developed. In addition, the ethics and characteristics of successful small business consultants are discussed. Part I is comprised of Chapters 1, 2 and 3.

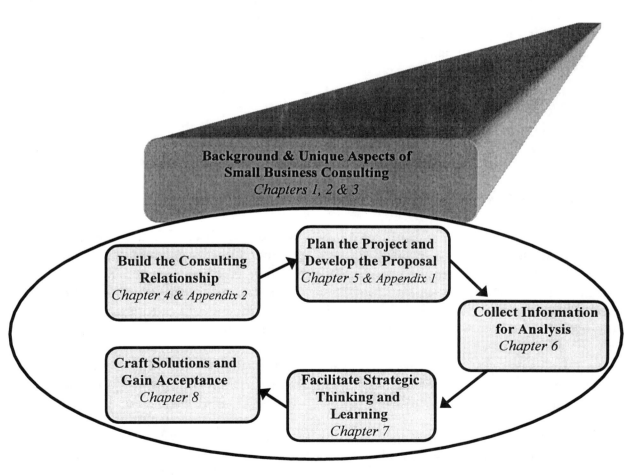

Chapter 1

Consulting To Small Business

This book will help management consultants meet the fast-growing need for small business consulting. In it, we describe research-based and experience-tested ways to develop and manage successful small business interventions. Dealing with small businesses is not like consulting "little big businesses" (Chowdhury and Lang, 1996) any more than piloting a jumbo jet is the same as flying a two-seater. In many ways, small businesses are unique, with special challenges, opportunities and needs. Thus, models and tools for intervening in large organizations, which tend to dominate the fields of management consulting and business in general, may not easily transfer to small businesses. This book focuses exclusively on the special case of small businesses, and offers ideas for helping the consultant's small business engagements take flight.

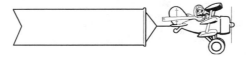

The Economic Impact of Small Business

Management consulting to small business is quietly becoming a major growth industry, albeit one that has received very little attention either in the research literature or the popular press. The growth is fueled by a proliferation of both the number of small businesses and their economic clout, and by the increasing dollars spent for management consulting services. The result of these trends is a corresponding need for management consultants with expertise in working with small organizations.

Consider the statistical evidence. Table 1-1 shows that over 99% of all businesses in the United States (U.S.) are classified as small* and that small businesses account for more than half of total U.S. business output and sales. During the 1990s, a period of

---

* The Small Business Administration (SBA) has established standards for classifying businesses by size. Different standards have been used depending on the industry (e.g., number of employees, sales volume). Number of employees, however, has been adopted by economists and government policy makers as the best standard to determine business size (*The Final Report,* 1995). Moreover, the SBA's Office of Advocacy has determined that a firm with *less than 500 employees* is considered small (*Issues Handbook,* 1995). This is the standard adopted in this book.

unprecedented big-business downsizing, the small business sector has realized a significant net increase in number of jobs, now accounting for over 54% of all private sector jobs in the United States. In contrast, large corporations have "restructured" and "downsized" to the point that the proportion of the American workforce employed by the Fortune 500 companies has dropped from 30% to 13% in just ten years (Drucker, 1995).

<u>Table 1-1</u>: **The Economic Impact of the Small Business Sector in the U.S.**

Economic Factor (Private Sector)	% of Total
Dollar Volume of Sales	52.0
Output	50.0
Employment	54.0
Employers	99.7
Business Assets	41.0

Source: *The Third Millennium: Small Business and Entrepreneurship in the 21st Century, 1995,* p 45.

Indeed, while large firms continue to capture most of the media attention, small businesses have been the engine of U.S. economic growth in recent years. The number of small businesses in the United States has increased 49% since 1982. Similarly, the number of new business start-ups per year has increased steadily during the past three decades and is expected to continue to increase into the next century. In 1994, new business incorporations reached an all-time high of 753,000; this represents a 5% gain over 1993 and 18% more than a decade earlier *(The Final Report, 1995).*

Job creation is one of the most significant contributions of the small business sector. From 1976 to 1990, 65% of net new jobs were created by small businesses; from 1989 to 1991 this number had jumped to 95% of net new jobs. Furthermore, according to the Small Business Administration, during the 1990s more than half of the new jobs paying $21 an hour or more were with small businesses (Byrd, 1995). Experts predict that small firms will continue to generate nearly all net new jobs well into the next century *(The Third Millennium: Small Business and Entrepreneurship in the 21st Century,* 1995), and that small organizations will employ over 70% of the U. S. workforce by the year 2000 (Chowdhury & Lang, 1996).

While the small business sector grows, so too does the demand for management consulting services. In the past ten years, the market for consulting services has more than doubled, to over $67 billion in annual revenues (Jackson, 1994). In 1994-95, revenue from consulting services was up 13.3% among the eight largest U.S. accounting firms. Indeed, if trends continue, "within three or four years the eight largest accountancy firms will earn more of their revenue from consultancy than from audit and accountancy -- they are in fact, less and less describable as accountancy firms" *(Firms Continue to Move Toward Consultancy, 1995).* While no statistics are available on the growth of consulting to small businesses, the combination of the growth of both the small business sector and the management consulting industry point to a trend. Indeed, a recent survey of over 1000 members of the Management Consulting Services Division of the American Institute of CPAs (AICPA) indicates that demand for consulting to small business is booming and no end is in sight *(Boom Year Seen for Small Business Consulting, 1995)*.

Purpose of the Book

This book is written for consultants who specialize in small business interventions and for students of management consulting. Its purpose is to develop and introduce frameworks and models for small business consulting and to describe practical tools and strategies for consulting. In so doing, we hope to fill a void in the field of management consulting by focusing on the unique challenges and opportunities of consulting to small businesses, including non-profits. Thus, the book is designed to be both theory-based and practical; it is grounded in the management consulting literature but it is also meant to be used as a fieldbook, offering experience-tested approaches for building successful small business interventions.

Management consulting is an important and complex activity. Accordingly, many practical books have been written about the consulting process. These books, however, are almost exclusively written from the perspective of consulting to large corporations. The demand for small business consulting is booming while research on the topic lags behind. An emerging need is to understand the consulting process, including tools and techniques of consulting, in the context of the small business setting.

Some of the concepts, frameworks and insights of consulting apply equally well to organizations of all sizes. In important ways, however, small businesses have unique needs, opportunities and limitations. The consultant who fails to recognize and adapt to these circumstances risks falling victim to a common mistake of treating the small business client as a large corporation. This book examines the process and practice of management consulting to small organizations, stressing the need to recognize and adapt to their special circumstances.

In this introductory chapter, we define key terms, provide a framework stressing key aspects of the small business consulting process, and provide an overview of the remaining chapters of the book.

Defining Key Terms

Three key terms in the book are: *small business, consulting, and project management*. In short, this is a book about using a project management approach to build successful consulting relationships with small organizations. The term *small organizations* rather than small business may be a more accurate description of our focus since the ideas, tools, and frameworks described apply to both for-profit and not-for -

profit enterprises. Indeed, we have used the models and tools described in the book to manage several consulting projects with non-profits, religious organizations, and social agencies. For the sake of consistency and simplicity, however, the term "small business" is used rather than small enterprise or small organizations.

Management consulting is the second key term, a concept that is not easy to define (in fact, a committee of consultants formed by the Arizona Society of Certified Public Accountants concluded that the term cannot be defined!) [Wilkinson, 1995, p 1-4]. Most consultants would agree, however, that the essence of management consulting is identifying and analyzing management needs, problems or opportunities, recommending courses of action to address the issues, and when requested, helping to implement the recommendations. Thus, consulting is a process of understanding and satisfying client needs.

The third term defining the core of the book is *project management.* Consulting projects typically go through a series of predictable stages of development, as we explain in chapter five. We have developed a four-stage model for project management, consisting of Exploration, Preparation, Implementation, and Conclusion (for the sake of easy recall, the *EPIC* Framework). The topic of project management for small business consulting is covered in-depth in chapter five and appendix one, and is a common thread throughout the book.

The need for a small business perspective on management consulting became increasingly evident to us during the course of our own teaching, research, consulting, and management experiences. An experienced-based appreciation of the uniqueness of the small business client is very difficult to find in the management literature, perhaps because the market for consulting to small business has been under-appreciated.

Sources of Information

Our ideas for this book come from several sources, including primary and secondary research, our own consulting experience, and our experience in teaching and mentoring students in management consulting courses. In terms of primary research, we have conducted focus group interviews and administered written surveys of more than 170 executives and undergraduate students during the mid-1990s. Each respondent was consulting a small business or non-profit at the time of the research. The results of these interviews and surveys, together with our discussions with others involved in the practice of small business consulting have been very helpful and, at the same time, confirmed our belief that research and recommendations on consulting to the small business client are scarce and needed.

We also base our ideas on secondary research, using a thorough review of the literature on management consulting. Computerized library searches were conducted of both print and electronic sources, and citations from these sources were used extensively.

A list of references is given at the conclusion of each chapter for readers interested in learning more about a particular topic.

Another source of ideas is our professional experience with consulting small organizations. While we have had the opportunity to work with organizations of all sizes, in recent years we find ourselves increasingly involved with small businesses and non-profit organizations. These experiences have proven to be very rich learning opportunities; however, all too often we have had to rely on intuition and trial and error because of the limited research available on the topic.

A final source has been our own undergraduate and Executive MBA students. For the past several years, we have had the privilege of being associated with talented groups of students and executives in management consulting courses that we teach. These students work in teams to complete a consulting project for a local organization, most of which are small businesses or social agencies. Our experience of guiding these projects has added to and reinforced our own knowledge.

Overview of the Book

A framework emphasizing various components of the small business consulting process is presented in Figure 1-1 on the following page. Each component of the framework is addressed in a chapter and/or appendix of the book.

As the framework shows, the first section of the book describes the background and uniqueness of small business consulting, and is comprised of chapters one, two, and three. This introductory chapter has established a foundation for the book by defining terms and introducing the components of the small business consulting process. An important first step is to recognize the nuances, constraints and special needs of the small business client. This topic is explored in chapter two. In chapter three, we examine the ethics and responsibilities of consulting to small businesses. Together, these chapters set the context for the remaining chapters.

Research suggests that relationships and team-building are paramount in small business interventions. Accordingly, the next component of Figure 1-1, and the focus of chapter four and appendix two, is building the client - consultant relationship. Using a team-building analogy, chapter four offers a model along with practical suggestions for building the consulting relationships so critical for success. In appendix two, five perspectives on small group facilitation are explained. This information may be used to manage the consultant's internal team process, to manage the relationship between the consultant and the client(s), or to facilitate the process of building high performing teams within the client organization.

The third component of the framework is project planning and management, topics covered in chapter five and appendix one. The EPIC Approach to managing small business interventions is described. Guidelines and tools for defining the project and managing its scope are presented, focusing particularly on ways to write a tight and coherent consulting proposal. Appendix one compares the features of several mid-level software programs appropriate for small business consulting projects.

Collecting information for small business consulting is the next step in the framework and is the focus of chapter six. A systematic process for organizing data collection, along with specific sources of information for small business consultants are identified. Electronic sources of information are emphasized.

Next, as shown in Figure 1-1, in chapter seven, we describe practical approaches for building a learning organization and facilitating strategic thinking in the client organization. We have encountered organizations with written strategic plans but no real sense of strategic thinking. Tools for developing this sense are described in this chapter.

The last component of the framework is to develop and deliver solutions that are embraced by the client. This is the focus of chapter eight. For each of the components of the framework, our intention is to provide a mix of both the theoretical underpinnings of the topic and the practical tools and strategies that get the job done.

Figure 1-1: Components of the Small Business Consulting Process

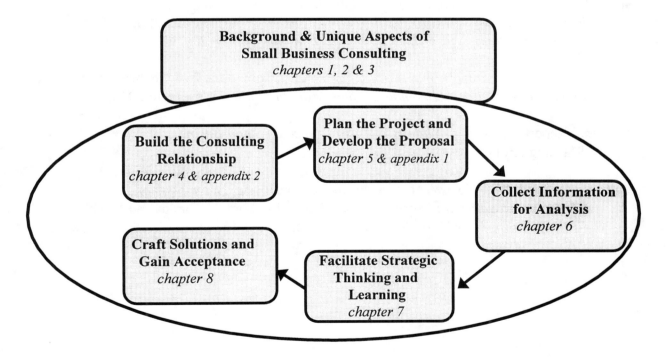

References

Boom Year Seen for Small Business Consulting. 1995. *The Practical Accountant*, 12.

Byrd, Jerry W. June 15, 1995. They're After Big Changes to Assist Small Business, *The Philadelphia Inquirer,* C1 - C2.

Chowdhury, S. D. & J. R. Lang. 1996. Turnaround in Small Firms: An Assessment of Efficiency Strategies, *Journal of Business Research*, 36, 169 - 178.

Drucker, Peter F. 1995. Interview: The Post-Capitalist Executive, *Managing in a Time of Great Change*, New York: Truman Talley Books/Dutton, 1 - 17.

Firms Continue to Turn Towards Consultancy. July 1995. *Journal of Accountancy.*

Issues Handbook - The White House Conference on Small Business. 1995. Office of Advocacy, U.S. Small Business Administration, Washington, D.C.

Jackson, Alan W. January 1994. How to Pick A Consultant, *Small Business Reports*, 9 - 12.

Survey on Trends and Future Developments in Management Consulting to Small Business, January 24, 1995. *Management Consulting Services Division of the American Institute of Certified Public Accountants,* Jersey City, NJ

The Third Millennium: Small Business and Entrepreneurship in the 21st Century. 1995. *Office of Advocacy, U.S. Small Business Administration*, Washington, D.C.

The Final Report. 1995. *The White House Conference on Small Business,* Washington, D.C.

Wilkinson, Joseph W. 1995. What is Management Consulting?, *Handbook of Management Consulting Services, 2nd edition.* Ed. Sam W. Barcus and Joseph W. Wilkinson. New York: McGraw-Hill, Inc. 1.3 - 1.16.

Chapter 2

Special Needs Of
The Small Business Client

The purpose of chapter two is to develop and propose a model for better understanding the nuances of management consulting to small business clients. The model identifies differences between consulting to small versus large clients, and also points out the related special needs of the small business.

The topic of small business consulting has received relatively little attention in the management consulting literature. A review of the literature does, however, reveal isolated descriptions of factors that differentiate small business consulting. The model proposed in this chapter collects these fragmented pieces and attempts to construct a unified and integrated perspective on the issue. From this model, a set of special client needs emerges and is identified in this chapter, and analyzed in-depth in subsequent chapters.

Factors Impacting Small Business Consulting: A Model

Our experience and research suggests that consulting interventions with small business clients are not the same as engagements with large corporations. The differences are a due to the distinct external environments and internal factors that affect large and small organizations differently.

The *external* factors include outside forces and trends that are impacting all small businesses. The second set of factors is *internal* to the organization but tend to be common among small business clients. Awareness of these factors is a requisite for success in consulting to small businesses. Figure 2-1 identifies the factors that impact the small business consultant and serves as a preliminary model for defining and planning for the special needs of a small business.

At the center of the model is the small business consultant (see Figure 2-1), operating in an environment that is constrained by the client's resource limitations and by certain management values and attitudes. The client, in turn, is dealing with a complex, rapidly changing external environment with its own set of barriers and constraints. These sets of factors create the special needs of the small business client, explained later in the chapter.

Figure 2-1: The Operating Environment of the Small Business Consultant

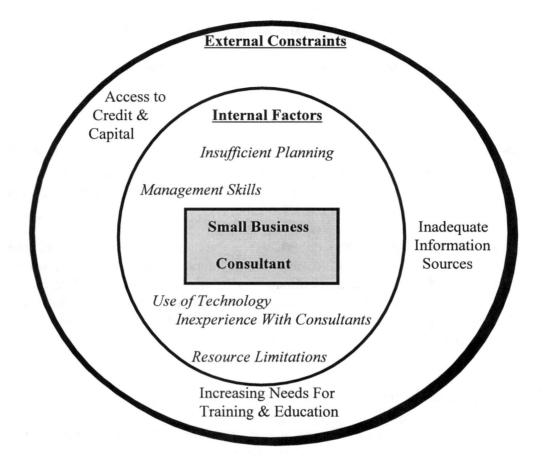

External Factors: Trends in Small Business

To assess the future of small business and entrepreneurship in the 21st century, the U.S. Small Business Administration, in cooperation with the White House Conference on Small Business and Professor David Brophy of the University of Michigan, held a series of focus groups during 1994 and 1995. The purpose of the focus group process was to tap into the insights, experiences, and perspectives of diverse groups of experts on small business issues (*The Third Millennium: Small Business and Entrepreneurship in the 21st Century*, 1995).

During 34 hours of discussions, the focus panel uncovered four dominant, interrelated themes or trends in small business, each affecting the small business consultant. The trends are rapid change, complexity, barriers to small business, and continued growth. Table 2-1 summarizes the four themes and provides insight into what the future holds for small businesses in the 21st century.

Table 2-1: Trends in Small Business

Theme One	**Rapid change** will continue and a sense of impermanence will grow. Our economy, our society, and the context for both large and small businesses are undergoing rapid and fundamental changes and these changes are expected to continue apace into the 21st century. The rapidity of change and its fundamental nature have engendered an essential sense of impermanence, which has brought into question some of the basic elements of how businesses, our society, and our economy operate.
Theme Two	**Heterogeneity, diversity, and complexity** will continue to be hallmarks of the small business sector. By history and by nature, the small business and entrepreneurial portion of the U.S. economy and society is a rich stew of diversity and complexity. Heterogeneity, diversity, and complexity, on the one hand, make generalizations about small business persons and entrepreneurs difficult, and, on the other hand are one of the reasons for the strengths and vitality of this sector of the economy.
Theme Three	**Barriers to small business** entry and inhibitors of growth are problematic. The focus groups identified the following factors: access to credit will be difficult, access to capital will continue to be a problem, an increasing need for effective training and education exits, and small businesses suffer from inadequate data, information and analysis.
Theme Four	**Continued strength** of the small business and entrepreneurial sector will be maintained. Despite the barriers to growth, small business and entrepreneurship will continue to grow and make major contributions in terms of job creation, innovation, empowerment, and self-realization, and will continue to embody the "American dream."

Source: *The Third Millennium: Small Business and Entrepreneurship in the 21st Century, 1995,* pp 4 - 17.

The confluence of these four trends creates a very dynamic operating environment which can be treacherous to navigate. Indeed, small business failure rates are notoriously high. Studies by the SBA have found that 63 percent of new businesses will fail within 6 years (Zimmerer and Scarborough, 1996). Of course, this figure reflects entrepreneurial ventures only, but small businesses, in general, suffer high mortality rates. Among the most common reasons cited for small business failures are:

- a lack of formal planning,
- insufficient market analysis,
- undercapitalization, and
- insufficient organization, structure, and written policies (Fields, 1995).

These issues are discussed below within the context of the explanation of Figure 2-1.

From a small business consulting viewpoint, Theme Three in Table 2-1 is of particular importance. Small business growth is restricted by:

- difficulties with gaining access to credit and capital,
- increasing needs for management training and development, and
- inadequate data, information and analysis.

These special challenges of the small business should be kept paramount in the consultant's mind and, accordingly, should be reflected in the design and execution of the consulting engagement. Brief explanations of each of these external constraints are described below.

Access To Credit & Capital. Commercial banks are risk averse when it comes to small business lending. The bankers we know and have dealt with half-jokingly admit that "small businesses are good loan prospects when they can demonstrate that they don't need a loan". Small businesses that critically need a line of credit are typically going to be turned down unless they can put up the necessary collateral. Venture capitalists and capital markets are another option, which may or may not be realistic depending on the nature of the organization.

Increasing Needs For Management Training. As markets become more complex, competitive and dynamic, the need for ongoing management training and development becomes ever more critical. Unfortunately for small business owners, taking time away for management development and education is often viewed as an expensive luxury.

Even at entry level positions, training is crucial. We were recently involved in a consulting intervention with a start-up premium bread bakery. To the owners great credit, he recognized the need for employee training in greeting and serving customers, creating a welcoming atmosphere, and maintaining the highest standards of product quality. These are extremely important and difficult standards to uphold in a retail business with part-time employees.

Inadequate Access to Information. For small businesses to compete effectively, they must have access to current, relevant information. However, an adequate system of economic data collection and distribution for small businesses does not exist (*The Third Millennium*, 1995). The problem, simply stated, is that small private businesses, unlike public corporations, are not required to disclose their financial statements. Managers are often at a loss as to where to find data, particularly competitive intelligence. Small business consultants create value for clients by providing information for strategic planning and decision-making.

One example of this problem involves a natural spring water company we encountered.. The company wanted a way to balance its cyclical business since most of its sales were in warm weather months. For years they toyed with the idea of entering the market for, of all products, windshield wiper fluid. Not having easy access to data to analyze the size and profit potential of the market, and not knowing how to gain it, they requested our assistance. Using techniques described in chapter six, we examined the size and structure of the market and easily concluded that this was not a viable line extension for the client.

Internal Factors: The Client

In addition to the external constraints described above, Figure 2-1 identifies a set of internal factors that are particularly relevant in small business consultations. Let's examine the these factors.

Consider the results of the AICPA survey of over 1000 management consultants, cited in chapter one. One question asked respondents about the differences between consulting to large versus small clients. Results indicated that smaller firms are less likely than their larger counterparts to have certain management policies and practices in place to help them improve the effectiveness or efficiency of their company. A particular disparity was found in areas such as being prepared to compete in the global market and having the ability to undertake strategic planning *(Survey on Trends and Future Developments in Management Consulting to Small Business,* 1995). Similarly, Krakoff & Fouss (1993) found that most small businesses do not possess mission statements, human resource policies, or even strategic plans for the future. Table 2-2 highlights some of the key differences between large and small firms according to the AICPA survey.

Table 2-2: Small Versus Large Business Clients

% of Respondents Indicating "All, Most or Many" Companies

	Under $3 million	$3 million or more
Perform long range planning	7.4 %	61.7%
Prepared to compete in a global market	2.5	43.2
Make good use of technology	37.2	81.6
Regularly evaluate cash management	27.8	80.5
Know how to use consultants	10.0	48.2

Source: *Survey on Trends and Future Developments in Management Consulting to Small Business, American Institute of CPAs, 1995, p 12.*

Use Of Technology. One of the internal factors in Figure 2-1 and listed above is making good use of technology. Technological changes have had a major impact on what small businesses can do, how they do it, and the efficiency with which they do it. It has allowed small firms to compete more effectively. There appears to be no end in sight for this revolution. It will continue to improve the capability and the opportunity of small businesses to form, serve, and compete in today's market. It is essential that small businesses continue to have meaningful access, at reasonable costs, to the so called "information highway" and its successors (*The Third Millennium*, 1995). Consultants have played, and will continue to play, a key role in making this happen.

A small plastics company we consulted is a case in point. The company had not changed its production process or technology in more than a decade. While its product continued to be viable, its cost structure became bloated as competitors adopted more cost-efficient production processes. After analyzing the situation, we determined that the company's owner was faced with the prospect of either making a large-scale investment in upgrading technology or closing the plant. He decided that the investment was too large to justify, given expected returns to the company.

Inexperience With Consultants. A second internal factor in Figure 2-1 and the last item in Table 2-2, is knowing how to use consultants. This factor presents one of the unique challenges of being a consultant to small business owner-managers. Compared to their larger counterparts, small businesses are inexperienced in using consultants, and sometimes inherently distrustful. According to some owners, the definition of a consultant is "someone who borrows your watch to tell you what time it is, and then keeps the watch as compensation".

Generally, owners of small businesses have built their own companies by a combination of skill, hard work, and frequently, some luck (Blackford, 1992). They tend to be extremely proud and fiercely independent (Pech and Mathew, 1993). As a result, some small business owners may view the use of a consultant as a sign of weakness and either refuse to seek or reluctantly seek their assistance. Like a doctor, a consultant is often not engaged until after the patient is obviously sick. Money for consulting is frequently not budgeted and tends to be scarce, and consultants may be perceived as an expensive option or a last resort (Pech, 1993).

Inexperience in using consultants may create other problems as well, such as engaging the consultant too late in the decision-making process. The AICPA survey of consultants to small business suggests ways that small business manager may make better use of consultants. Results of the survey are shown in Table 2-3.

Table 2-3: Using Small Business Consultants More Effectively

	% of Respondents Offering the Advice
Plan ahead to use consultants	40.0%
Contact consultants early in decision-making	21.6
Consider consultants part of management/ use consultants for business planning	12.0
Communicate/ ask questions	10.0

Source: *Survey on Trends and Future Developments in Management Consulting to Small Business, 1995, p 15.*

Management Skills. Small business owner/managers often have inordinate demands on them, such as being expected to be CEO, CFO, VP Marketing, and chief strategist all in one. Unfortunately as we know, a jack of all trades may be a master on none. Small business owners rarely have the functional expertise in all areas required to operate a business (Pech and Mathew, 1993). Additionally, they may lack a skilled or experienced staff to help them (Blackford, 1992). Studies have found that lack of experience and management incompetence are two leading causes of small business failure (Zimmerer and Scarborough, 1996).

In recent years, we have been increasingly involved in consulting interventions with non-profits and religious institutions. The directors of these institutions usually lack any formal business education, but compensate with their passion and commitment for advancing a social or religious cause. Management skills are learned on-the-job, if at all. Many of these directors recognize their need for management development.

Limits on Resources. As previously mentioned, a major cause of small business failure is inadequate (or nonexistent) financial planning, and undercapitalization. The lack of capital leaves small companies with little cushion against major outside shocks or their own errors, and makes them especially vulnerable to financial crises (Blackford, 1992). Also, the size of the small business owner's revenue base frequently means that he or she does not have the resources to hire consultants when assistance is needed (Pech and Mathew, 1993). A budget allocation earmarked specifically for outside consultants is the exception in small business.

Social agencies and non-profits are especially vulnerable to limited resources. Without exception, the agencies we have consulted are under-resourced and their directors are alarmed by the daunting challenge of providing more services during an era of federal government cutbacks in social programs. Fund raising, grant writing, and corporate sponsorship are at the forefront of every director's mind.

Insufficient Planning. One common problem for small business owners is that time and attention are often spread across too many responsibilities and areas, leading to a short-term orientation. Some entrepreneurs and small business managers are so preoccupied with day-to-day operations, there is a tendency to get buried in details (Woodard, 1992). This can lead to insufficient time spent on strategic planning. Research indicates that lack of time to engage in planning is one of the main reasons for small business failures (Nahavandi and Chesteen, 1988). This problem was confirmed in the AICPA survey of consultants who indicated that "small businesses are too caught-up in day-to-day operations, without sufficient focus on strategic planning" *(Survey on Trends and Future Developments in Management Consulting to Small Business,* 1995, p 14). The single most important piece of advice the survey respondents could offer small business managers was to plan ahead and use long-term strategic planning. Other commonly-mentioned responses are presented in Table 2-4 on the following page.

Table 2-4: **Consultants' Single Most Important Advice to Small Businesses**

Advice	% of Respondents Offering the Advice
Use strategic planning	34.2%
Communicate your concerns	12.1
Control cash flow	8.3
Know when consulting services are needed	7.6

Source: *Survey on Trends and Future Developments in Management Consulting to Small Business, 1995, p 14.*

Special Needs Of The Small Business Client

The unique features of the operating environment of the small business consultant, pictured in the model of Figure 2-1 and described above, create special client needs. In particular, we stress four special needs:

- access to data,
- strategic thinking and learning,
- project management,
- the client/consultant relationship.

The need for access to industry and competitive data, and the need for strategic planning, thinking and learning have been described in the preceding sections. Below we examine more closely the remaining two needs.

Project Planning & Management

According to William Reeb (1993), the small business client needs consulting services characterized by customization, speed, simplicity, cost control, and creative delivery systems. These are outcomes of a systematic approach to planning and managing the intervention, which we refer to as *project management.*

Small businesses need *customized* solutions tailored to the unique circumstances and resource capability of the firm. Prepackaged and one-size-fits-all answers that may sell in the large corporation are useless to the small business. *Speed* to decision-making is another key. Solutions that are relatively *simple*, easy to implement and inexpensive will be more likely to be embraced. In addition, *costs* must be controlled. This may require *creativity in both project design and delivery* -- one key to operating profitably with small businesses is to design and tailor the delivery of the project to the budgetary needs of the client. Clients may be unable to afford to pay the consultant to perform the entire project but the consultant can design the project in stages, some parts to be completed by the consultant and others by the client organization. When money is very scarce, the consultant can shift from the role of performing the project to planning the project and turning it back to the client for completion. These techniques are described in chapter five. Taken as a whole Reeb's primary emphasis is on efficiency in project management.

Building The Client/Consultant Relationship

The AICPA survey also sheds light on the special interests of the small business client. Table 2-5 shows the attributes of consultants most valued by small business managers, according to survey results.

Quality of services, reputation, and personal attention or "chemistry" were ranked first more than any other attributes, highlighting the essential nature of the client/consultant relationship. Indeed, the study concludes:

> these findings confirm that while technical expertise and reputation are important, the "soft side" - the personal nature of the client-consultant relationship - is also critical.... reputations and relationships may well be an important differentiating factor when (small) companies are looking for consulting services *(Survey on Trends*, p 14).

Table 2-5: **What Small Businesses Value in a Consultant**

Attribute	% of Respondents Indicating "Most Important"
Quality of services	23.7%
Reputation	23.1
Personal attention or "chemistry"	15.6
Industry Expertise	15.2
Usefulness of Information	7.1
Knowledge of their company	4.4
Impact on bottom line	4.4
Timeliness of service	3.6
Reasonable fees	2.0

Another viewpoint on the special needs of the small business client is offered by Fields (1995) who also emphasizes client/consultant rapport. In addition, Fields encourages the consultant to be focused, in fact, to be "more focused than your client by paying special attention to each of the firm's functional areas" and by helping the firm to focus on its mission and objectives (pp 137 - 138). The consultant should know more about the company than the owner, says Fields, and should get involved in implementing recommendations, not just developing them and handing them off.

The four special needs are shown in Figure 2-2 on the following page as an outcome of the unique operating environment of the small business consultant. The model implies that one key to successful small business consultations is for consultants to understand these needs and adapt their intervention styles and approaches accordingly.

Conclusion

Both the number and economic clout of small businesses in the United States have been growing rapidly. Despite these trends, relatively little has been written about the unique challenges and opportunities of small business consulting. A review of the literature and our own consulting experience suggests several key factors that differentiate small and large clients. While various authors have emphasized key differences, no previous study has attempted to collect these fragmented pieces and construct a unified model of small business consulting. The model proposed in this study is an effort to fill this void. The model stresses differences at both the client level and in the external environment of the small business client. A corresponding set of special client needs arises from these differences. In later chapters we focus specifically on these client needs (see Figure 2-2) and offer advice for addressing them. Recognizing and adapting to these needs, it is argued, is an important consideration for the consultant.

Figure 2-2: **Special Needs of the Small Business Client**

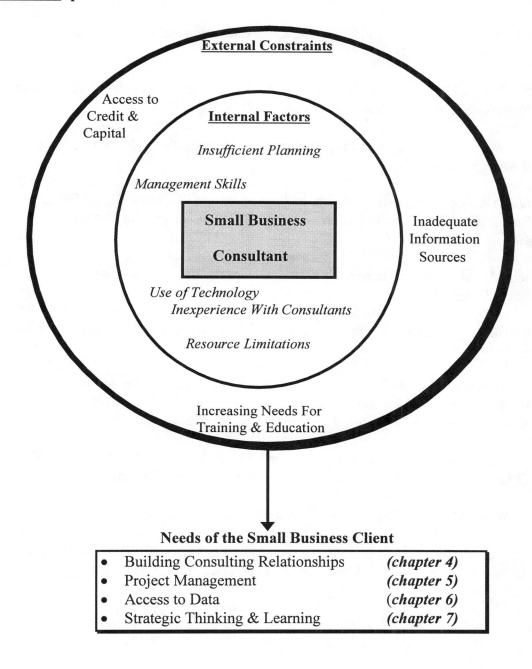

Needs of the Small Business Client

• Building Consulting Relationships	*(chapter 4)*
• Project Management	*(chapter 5)*
• Access to Data	*(chapter 6)*
• Strategic Thinking & Learning	*(chapter 7)*

References

Blackford, John. 1992. Consulting to Smaller Companies. *Journal of Management Consulting, 7: 25 - 28.*

Fields, W. Calvin. 1995. Effective Small Business Consultants Are Focused, ***Journal of Professional Services Marketing,*** Vol. 12 (2), 127 - 143.

Krakoff, R. & J. Fouss. 1993. Defining the Small Business Market, ***Marketing Research,*** 5, 28 - 31.

Nahavandi, Afsaneh and Chesteen, Susan. 1988. The Impact of Consulting on Small Business: A Further Examination. *Entrepreneurship Theory and Practice,* 29-40.

Pech, Richard J. and Alistar Mathew. Spring 1993. Critical Factors for Consulting to Small Business, *Journal of Management Consulting,* 61 - 63.

Reeb, William L. August 1993. Can Small Business Consulting Be Profitable?, *Journal of Accountancy,* 54 - 56.

Survey on Trends and Future Developments in Management Consulting to Small Business, January 24, 1995. *Management Consulting Services Division of the American Institute of Certified Public Accountants,* Jersey City, NJ

The Third Millennium: Small Business and Entrepreneurship in the 21st Century. 1995. *Office of Advocacy, U.S. Small Business Administration,* Washington, D.C.

Woodard, Wiley M. 1992. Help Wanted. ***Black Enterprise,*** 2: 219-222.

Zimmerer, Thomas W. & Scarborough, Norman M. 1996. *Effective Small Business Management, 5th edition.* Upper Saddle River, NJ: Prentice Hall, Inc.

Chapter 3

Ethics And Responsibilities

The small business consultant operates in a unique environment as described in chapter two. This uniqueness, in turn, has important implications for the roles and responsibilities performed, and the skills and traits required of the consultant. The purpose of this chapter is to describe the roles and responsibilities of small business consultants in light of the special features of their operating environment. We begin with a discussion of the ethics of consulting.

Consulting Ethics

Like other professions such as law and medicine, the management consulting profession has its own code of ethics. A professional code of ethics serves several purposes. It educates the members of the profession as to the types of practices, decisions and ethical conduct that serve and protect the interests of both clients and consultants. Experience has shown that following the standards of the code is one important way to retain public trust and confidence. The code may also serve as a visible, objective standard by which consultants can weigh and evaluate their decisions.

There is more than one version of the consultant's code of ethics, although different versions are similar in many respects. The American Institute of Certified Public Accountants (AICPA) has compiled a set of ethical standards for management consulting while other organizations, including the Institute of Management Consultants (IMC) and the Association of Management Consulting Firms (ACME) have jointly developed a code of ethics focusing on four issues - clients, engagements, fees, and the profession. Table 3-1 on the following page presents this code of ethics. Those who represent themselves as consultants are expected to know and abide by these standards, regardless of whether they belong to any of the aforementioned professional organizations (Cherrington, 1995).

Qualities Of An Effective Consultant

To understand the characteristics of an effective small business consultant, we first examine the literature in this area as it relates to consulting in general, regardless of the size of the client, and then zero-in on the unique and/or modified roles and responsibilities of the small business consultant. By using this approach, we can recognize the qualities of successful consultants common to all settings but also identify the circumstances and the specialized skills and characteristics needed in the small business context.

Table 3-1: Code Of Ethics for Management Consultants

Clients

1. We will serve our clients with integrity, competence, and objectivity.

2. We will keep client information and records of client engagements confidential and will use proprietary client information only with the client's permission.

3. We will not take advantage of confidential client information for ourselves or our firms.

4. We will not allow conflicts of interest which provide a competitive advantage to one client through our use of confidential information from another client who is a direct competitor without that competitor's permission.

Engagements

5. We will accept only engagements for which we are qualified by our experience and competence.

6. We will assign staff to client engagements in accordance with their experience, knowledge, and expertise.

7. We will immediately acknowledge any influence on our objectivity to our clients and will offer to withdraw from a consulting engagement when our objectivity or integrity may be impaired.

Fees

8. We will agree independently and in advance on the basis for our fees and expenses and will charge fees and expenses that are reasonable, legitimate, and commensurate with the services we deliver and the responsibility we accept.

9. We will disclose to our clients in advance any fees or commissions that we will receive for equipment, supplies, or services we recommend to our clients.

Profession

10. We will respect the intellectual property rights of our clients, other consulting firms, and sole practitioners and will not use proprietary information or methodologies without permission.

11. We will not advertise our services in a deceptive manner and will not misrepresent the consulting profession, consulting firms, or sole practitioners.

12. We will report violations of the Code of Ethics.

According to Shenson (1990), effective consultants possess special knowledge, talents, and skills. Adapting this typology, we develop a framework for the qualities of effective consultants based on their *knowledge, skills, and traits*. Table 3-2 shows four viewpoints on the question presented in the knowledge, skill, trait framework.

Table 3-2: **Qualities of an Effective Consultant**

	J. Owen Cherrington (1)	Larry E. Greiner and Robert O. Metzger (2)	Howard L. Shenson (3)	Geoffrey M. Bellman (4)
Knowledge:	Education, Training and/or Experience Intelligence	Knowledge		Expertise
Skills:	Communication Problem-Solving Judgment Objectivity Understands People	Communication Solution Skills Managerial Skills Diagnostic Ability Marketing & Sales	Precision and Persuasiveness Sense of Relevance Comprehensiveness Foresight Lingual Sophistication Fact consciousness	Perspective
Traits:	Empathy Integrity Courage Psychological Maturity Ambition Energetic	Personality Attributes Conducive to Consulting,	Self-Discipline	Authenticity Friendship

Sources: (1) *Professional Attributes for Consultants*, 1995
(2) *Consulting to Management*, 1983.
(3) *How to Select and Manage Consultants*, 1990.
(4) *The Consultant's Calling*, 1990.

Cherrington provides a clear and detailed description of the qualities needed to be an effective consultant. Knowledge and technical training provide the foundation for the consultant. Also, a wide range of personal attributes that make an individual amiable to people and effective in accomplishing desirable objectives through people is emphasized.

Greiner and Metzger, like Cherrington, provide a multi-faceted analysis of a consultant's qualities. They too emphasize knowledge and "personality attributes conducive to consulting" which they define to include ethical standards, empathy and trust, positive thinking, self-motivation, team player, self-fulfillment, mobility, energy, and self-awareness. Greiner and Metzger's philosophy is that if the consultant is not perceptive, does not communicate with sensitivity, or lacks up-to-date knowledge, the client's problems will not be solved.

Shenson's description is abstract and requires further explanation. Table 3-3 defines each of his qualities.

Table 3-3: **Shenson's View of the Effective Consultant**

QUALITY	DEFINITION
Fact Consciousness	An insistence upon getting the facts and checking their accuracy.
Sense of Relevance	The capacity to recognize what is relevant to the issue at hand and to cut away irrelevant facts, opinions, and emotions that can cloud an issue.
Comprehensiveness	The capacity to see all sides of a problem, the many different factors that bear upon it, and the variety of possible ways of approaching it.
Foresight	The capacity to take the long view, to anticipate remote and collateral consequences, to look several moves ahead in the particular chess game that is being played.
Lingual Sophistication	An ability to see beyond words and catch phrases; a refusal to accept verbal solutions that merely conceal the problem.
Precision and Persuasiveness	A mastery of the language, which includes the ability to state what one means, no more and no less, and the ability to convey one's ideas to other people to convince them of the wisdom of those ideas.
Self-Discipline	A commitment to thoroughness and an abhorrence of superficiality and approximation.

Source: *How to Select and Manage Consultants*, p 6.

Shenson's emphasis is clearly and emphatically on the cognitive skills of the consultant, especially on the ability to accurately diagnose and conceptualize, using the analytical tools needed to comprehend and resolve problems. He pays relatively little attention to the interpersonal qualities that Cherrington, and Greiner and Metzger highlight. Shenson's views, however, do not contradict the other authors. In fact, he complements them by limiting his focus to the analytical skills of consulting, but exploring them in greater depth. The scope of his analysis is more narrow but also deeper.

Bellman's terminology is also unique and requires further explanation. Table 3-4 on the following page gives brief explanations of his qualities. A closer analysis of Bellman's contribution reveals that while his terminology is new, his message is consistent with the Cherrington, and Greiner and Metzger models. Overall, Bellman concludes that knowledge, communication, and client trust are the most important qualities of an effective consultant.

Table 3-4: **Bellman's View of the Effective Consultant**

QUALITIES	EXPLANATION
Expertise	Extensive knowledge in a particular area.
Perspective	New vision, viewpoints, and alternatives. Creativity, leading to new actions.
Authenticity	Be what you are, not something else. If you are a phony the client will take offense and not use your services.
Friendship	A solid client-consultant relationship is based on friendship. It builds trust.
Accomplishment	Achieve results! It is the ultimate marketing tool.

Source: *The Consultant's Calling,* pp 127-139.

Each of these four studies sheds light on the attributes of effective consultants. A careful analysis of each model reveals a significant amount of consistency and convergence on a core set of themes. Indeed, a synthesis of the four models seems to produce five overlapping attributes of the effective consultant: (1) expertise, (2) communication skills, (3) problem-solving abilities, (4) integrity and ethics, and (5) interpersonal skills. Table 3-5 on the next page shows the relationship between the authors' views and the five emergent themes. The five attributes are developed in the section that follows.

Qualities Of An Effective Small Business Consultant

Table 3-5 and the analysis above highlight the qualities needed by the effective consultant, regardless of the size of the client being served. With this information as a context, we now turn to the particular case of the small business consultant.

The same five attributes needed to be an effective consultant distilled from the analysis above - *expertise, communication, problem-solving, ethics, and interpersonal skills* - are also critical in the context of small business consulting. In the case of the small business, however, there are subtle but important distinctions. According to consultant and author Curt Kampmeier (1996):

> The type of management consultant who is right for a public company is often not right at all for the business owner. Where the public company often wants a feasibility study, or a system or program of some sort, the business owner typically wants a long-term relationship with an advisor who can offer counsel on a continuing basis. (p 21).

Kampmeier goes on to describe the special characteristics of management consultants "who are most effective in working with business owners". His views are reflected in the following paragraphs, beginning with the cornerstone of small business consulting success -- relationships and interpersonal skills.

Table 3-5: **A Synthesis: Attributes of the Effective Consultant**

ATTRIBUTE	Cherrington (1)	Greiner and Metzger (2)	Shenson (3)	Bellman (4)
1. Expertise	Education, Training and/or Experience Intelligence	Knowledge		Expertise
2. Communication	Communication Skills	Communication Skills	Precision and Persuasiveness	
3. Problem-Solving	Problem-Solving Ability Judgment Objectivity	Solution Skills Diagnostic Ability	Sense of Relevance Comprehensiveness Foresight Lingual Sophistication Fact Consciousness	Perspective Accomplish-ment
4. Integrity & Ethics	Integrity Psychological Maturity Courage	Ethical	Self-Discipline	Authenticity
5. Interpersonal Skills	Empathy Understanding of People	Empathy & Trust Team Player		Friendship

Adapted from: (1) *Professional Attributes for Consultants*, 1995
                           (2) *Consulting to Management*, 1983.
                           (3) *How to Select and Manage Consultants*, 1990.
                           (4) *The Consultant's Calling*, 1990.

Interpersonal Skills

A constant theme throughout the book is the paramount importance of relationships in the small business consultation. Owners and small business managers need consultants who are more interested in long-term relationships than in a one-time project (Kampmeier, 1996). Indeed, the entire focus of the next chapter is building this type of long-term consulting relationship. We believe that the team analogy is a useful one to apply to the client - consultant relationship. Each player in the team has goals which are satisfied in a mutually beneficial relationship.

Small business clients need to know they can trust the judgment and motives of the consultant. The consultant, in turn, needs time to understand the client's goals, values and constraints. This long-term orientation may affect both the types of recommendations and solutions proposed by the consultant, as well as the terms and conditions of the consulting agreements.

Expertise

Consultants are expected to be in the forefront of knowledge in their fields of expertise (Greiner and Metzger, 1983). In the case of small business consultants, knowledge should be both broad and deep according to Kampmeier (1996). The business owner knows well his or her company, and perhaps a few others. But the consultant needs to have insight into hundreds of companies, not just a few. This breadth and depth of expertise allows the consultant to identify and exploit unique opportunities but also to see common patterns where proven solutions may be adapted to the client's situation. At the same time, the small business consultant does not portend to be all things to all people. They are "expert enough to respond to a few areas themselves and to make a real contribution, but they do not practice outside their areas of specialization" (p 22). Rather, they use their networks to introduce the small business client to other consultants with the required expertise.

Consultants to small business must also be grounded in proven business basics and wary of the management fads that are so readily embraced by larger corporations. As Kampmeier (1996) points out, trendy new ideas that promise a quick fix for complex problems are "dangerously simplistic" for the small business. While remaining on the cutting-edge of consulting knowledge, the small business consultant needs to stay focused on the tried and true problem-solving approaches.

Communication

Another attribute of the effective consultant described above is effective communication. An accurate interchange of information, thoughts, opinions and feelings between individuals is a critical skill for all consultants (Cherrington, 1995), including the ability to effectively speak, write, and listen. In the small business setting, the consultant must not only possess these communication skills, but also be a "straight shooter" (Kampmeier, 1996). Small business consultants must have the freedom and courage to challenge the assumptions and perceptions of the owner/manager. Reticence with the client out of fear of losing business is never in the best interests of the client. In the long-run, being a "straight-shooter" will help to build trust and foster the type of personal relationships so valued by the client.

Problem-Solving

Consulting is all about problem-solving. In the initial stages of a consulting engagement, underlying causes of the client's problem are often unknown. The consultant must search the evidence, read the clues, and define the problems (Greiner and Metzger, 1983).

As will be discussed in chapter eight, creativity is an element of problem-solving and is at a premium when dealing with the small business manager. Creativity not only in diagnosing problems and developing solutions, as would be expected in any consulting situation, but creativity in both the design and execution of the consulting project so as to reflect the budget and resource constraints of the client.

The most perplexing issues faced by the small business client, according to Kampmeier (1996), are rarely resolved by number-crunching and quantitative analysis. Rather "qualitative analysis", based on reasoned judgment, wisdom, and fresh insights are needed. This implies that the consultant must be "willing to run the risk of being wrong in order to act with the speed and decisiveness that enterprising situations demand." Small business consultants must be prepared to provide "a professional judgment that comes from experience... and not just from the numbers" (p 22).

Integrity and Ethics

The final attribute of the small business consultant, integrity and ethics, is a natural extension of our emphasis on interpersonal relationships. Attributes that make up integrity include moral and ethical soundness, fairness, honesty, and dependability. These attributes form the basic philosophies behind the code of ethics presented at the beginning of this chapter. Lack of integrity is damaging in any consultant-client relationship but potentially devastating in the small business environment. Since most small businesses have little slack in their operations, the actions of an unethical consultant could prove costly, even fatal, to the small company.

Types Of Consultants

The management consulting literature cites several different types of consultants. Some are more common among small businesses than others. Table 3-6 highlights two standard classifications of the types. These types are first described, then analyzed to identify which are most suitable for small businesses.

Table 3-6: Types of Consultants

Greiner and Metzger (1)	Kinard (2)
Generalist vs Specialist	Generalist vs Specialist
Process vs Content	Process vs Content
Diagnostic vs Implementation	Diagnostic vs Full-Process
Custom vs Packaged	Customized vs Packaged
Internal vs External	
Large Firm vs Small Firm	

Sources: (1) *Consulting to Management*, pp 18-26.
(2) *Handbook of Management Consulting Services, 2nd Edition*, pp 2-18 & 2-19.

Greiner and Metzger and Kinard offer almost identical descriptions of the types of consultants. The difference between a generalist and a specialist is typically a difference in breadth versus depth. Both types have special expertise but the generalist is more apt to work on broader, business-wide or cross-functional projects such as strategic planning and change management. The analytical tools of the generalist are believed to be relevant across most industry and organizational types. A *generalist* possesses knowledge about all functional business areas, usually through MBA training and professional experience. They are equipped to tackle a broad range of client problems.

The *specialist*, on the other hand, focuses on one area of expertise in great depth. Instead of tackling a broad range of problems, a specialist is trained to handle specific, usually more technical problems. This approach is an outgrowth of the tremendous expansion of knowledge and complexity of business. Typical examples include tax and regulatory consultants, and information systems specialists.

The difference between process and content consulting is more a matter of approach or methods than anything else. *Process* consultants encourage their clients to identify their own problems and formulate their own solutions through a series of questions and guidance. Process consultants facilitate the client's efforts, rather than offering their own solutions. Like a counselor, a process consultant teaches the client a sound problem-solving procedure.

An appropriate analogy for *content* consultants is a surgeon, in that they take a direct approach to diagnose the problem and develop a corrective action. The consultant performs all the phases in the process, relying heavily on his or her own knowledge, skills, and talents, and eventually, presenting a preferred solution to the client. Of course, the content and process approaches need not be seen as mutually exclusive and, indeed, their use may need to coincide to successfully complete a particular engagement.

The *diagnostic* approach identifies the causes of problems and recommends a course of action to solve the problem. However, this process stops short at this point and does not see the recommended changes through to fruition. The *full-process* approach, also called the *implementation* approach, includes the actual execution of the proposed changes.

The *custom* approach offers tailor-made solutions to each client's particular problem. The solution is a unique, one-of-a-kind product. The *packaged* approach emphasizes the similarities among problems faced by all companies. It attempts to offer a packaged methodology and a packaged solution that has been developed for a general set of problems. The Boston Consulting Group's "Growth/Share Matrix" is one example of a packaged approach to strategic planning.

The difference between *internal* and *external* consultants is simply that the internal consultant is an employee (usually full-time) of the company for which they provide their services while the external consultant is either an independent contractor or employed by another organization. Similarly, consultants may be classified according to the size of their firm. *Large* consulting firms, like the Big 6 accounting firms, tend to provide a wide range of services, usually at a premium price. *Small* firms and independent individual consultants tend to tackle smaller projects, offer more personal and customized service, but lack the resources of the larger firms.

Types Of Small Business Consultants

In considering these different types of consultants, small businesses need both generalists and specialists. If the owner of a small company knows that he or she has specific and especially technical needs, then it is best to use a specialist (e.g., a company needs assistance with the development of an information system). However, as we have discussed in chapter two, strategic thinking is often a deficiency in small businesses, a problem which can be addressed with a generalist consultant. In addition, when small businesses are unsure of their needs or problems, the services of a generalist may help them identify their problems and implement solutions.

Both process and content consulting, and diagnostic and implementation approaches, may be appropriate in the small business context, depending on the situation and the client's budget. When funds for consultants are limited, the content and diagnostic approaches may be favored since the content approach is more direct and may reduce overall billable hours, and, likewise, the diagnostic approach leaves the implementation step for the client. Furthermore, a custom solution is typically the best alternative for a small business. It may provide the company with a unique solution that can be used to create competitive advantage.

Internal consultants are more likely to be found in large corporations where projects are ongoing and resources to support consultants are more plentiful. The small firm compensates by hiring an external consultant but developing the long-term relationship discussed earlier, whereby the consultant is repeatedly engaged by the client. Finally, a small business is more likely to employ the services of a small consulting firm because of its needs for personalized service and cost containment.

Consulting Intervention Strategies

Several alternative strategies or styles of intervening in the client organization are available to the consultant. The choice of an appropriate intervention strategy will depend on the client's circumstances. Greiner and Metzger (1983) and Blake and Mouton (1983) offer similar conceptions of the intervention styles, as shown in Table 3 - 7 on the next page.

The *emotional* and *acceptant* styles of intervention are analogous. The consultant's role, in a nonjudgmental way, is to help the client clarify and accept his or her feelings about a concern, conflict, or issue. The purpose of the approach is to allow the client to express and release emotional energy to allow further movement. This strategy is appropriate when clients' emotions are clouding their judgment and perception, or hampering progress in some way.

Table 3-7: **Intervention Strategies**

Greiner & Metzger (1)	Blake & Mouton (2)
Emotional	Acceptant
Directional	Catalytic
Knowledge	Prescriptive
	Theory/ Principles
	Confronting

Sources: (1) *Consulting to Management*, pp 280-281.
                (2) cf. Rashford & Coughlan, 1994, pp 108 - 112..

The *catalytic* or *directional* strategy is the basis for all other approaches. This style of intervention is very process-oriented in that the consultant assumes the role of facilitator, and uses a series of questions and prompts to encourage clients to recognize situations and problems, and to develop their own solutions. The goal is to help the client define and validate the situation, allow the client to make a free and informed choice, and foster client commitment to the choice (Rashford & Coughlan, 1994).

In contrast, the *knowledge* style (or using Blake and Mouton's terminology, the *prescriptive* approach), is more content-oriented. That is, the consultant takes a direct approach to diagnosing the problem and developing solutions. This intervention strategy is appropriate when the client lacks time, information and/or expertise. Similarly, using the theory and principle style, the client is helped to see cause and effect relationships through the introduction of theoretical models.

A *confronting* style is used to directly challenge the assumptions, behaviors and/or decisions of the client. This approach is less common than the others but can be appropriate and effective, if used prudently. If it is misused, however, it can damage the client - consultant relationship which is so important in a small business intervention.

Thus, no single intervention style is appropriate for all clients and all circumstances. Furthermore, a particular consultation may require several different styles of intervention during the course of its life cycle. The small business consultant should cultivate and employ different styles as circumstances warrant.

Conclusion

In the previous chapter, we identified the special needs of the small business client. The corresponding roles, responsibilities and ethical standards of small business consulting are discussed in this chapter.

The first three chapters of this book have provided a foundation for understanding the unique aspects of consulting to small business. In the next four chapters, we will turn our attention to the special needs of the small business client. Each chapter will focus on and examine in-depth a particular special need.

References

Bellman, Geoffrey, M. 1990. *The Consultant's Calling*. San Francisco: Jossey-Bass.

Blake, R and Mouton, J. 1983. *Consultation, 2nd Edition*. Reading, MA: Addison-Wesley.

Cherrington, J. Owen 1995. Professional Attributes for Consultants. *Handbook of Management Consulting Services, 2nd Edition.* New York: McGraw-Hill.

Greiner, Larry E. and Metzger, Robert O. 1983. *Consulting to Management.* Englewood Cliffs: Prentice-Hall.

Kampmeier, Curt. May 1996. How To Get And Keep More Business Owners. *Journal of Management Consulting,* 21 - 23.

Kinard, James C. 1995. The Management Consulting Profession and Consulting Services. *Handbook of Management Consulting Services, 2nd Edition.* New York: McGraw-Hill.

Rashford, Nicholas S. and David Coghlan. 1994. *The Dynamics of Organizational Levels: A Change Framework for Managers and Consultants.* Reading, MA: Addison-Wesley.

Shenson, Howard L. 1990. *How to Select and Manage Consultants*. Lexington: Lexington Books.

PART II:

Special Needs of the Small Business Client

In Part II, we turn our attention to the special needs of the small business client. Chapters 4 through 7, along with Appendices 1 and 2, each focus on one of the special needs identified in Part I. Chapter 8 discusses theory and strategies for crafting solutions that are embraced by the client.

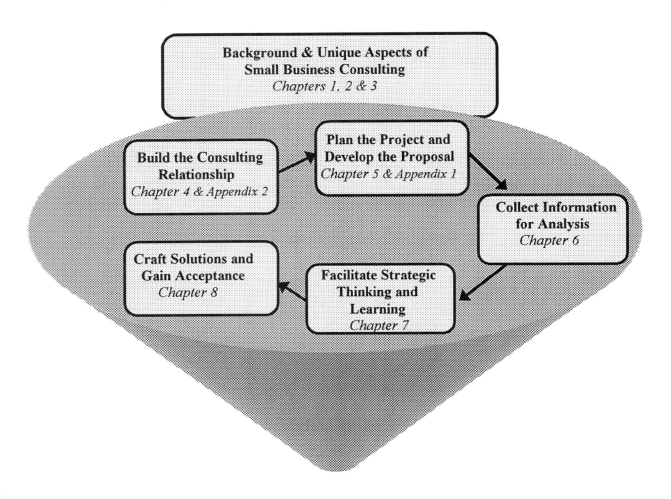

Chapter 4

Building a Consulting Relationship

In the first three chapters, we have described the special features of management consulting in a small business context. Small businesses and non-profits are faced by constraints (and opportunities) that large corporations do not typically encounter. We have identified the special needs that these differences create.

Among the most critical of these needs is the importance of building a strong client/consultant relationship, based on mutual trust. Studies indicate that personal relationships are a paramount consideration in the small business person's choice of a consultant. As Kampmeier (1996) argues, the small business owner typically wants a long-term relationship with a consultant who can offer counsel on an ongoing basis. The purpose of chapter four is to examine this concept in detail and to offer guidelines for building a constructive consulting practice based on mutually rewarding relationships.

This discussion of building a consulting relationship is based on the premise that a business interaction, and particularly a small business intervention, can be conceptualized as a *cooperative* or *collaborative* endeavor between individuals who expect mutual benefit from that interaction. This premise leads one to view small business consulting as a team-building effort, rather than a competitive endeavor. Therefore, team-building skills are critical for the business consultant. This is especially true for small businesses because they do not have authority over large numbers of employees nor do they have the reputation and financial resources of a large business. As a consequence, small businesses must secure assistance through networking, team-building, or other mutually beneficial, cooperative associations.

Since the popularization of Darwin's theory of evolution and the concept of natural selection, the competitive paradigm has been used far more extensively to explain business practices than has the cooperative paradigm. Yet team-building, teamwork and teams are pervasive in business.

This chapter explores small business consulting from the perspective of cooperation and team-building. A small group or team development framework that can be used in managing consulting interventions is described. By understanding the developmental stages through which a group of individuals progresses, it is possible to increase the probability of team success and reduce the amount of time spent on a project. But first let us begin by examining the team-building factors that are essential to successful small business consulting.

Managing Consulting Relationships: A Team-Building Perspective

Stated simply, *a successful consulting intervention is successful teamwork!* Consulting requires building a high-performing team. In this case the team consists of individuals from both the client organization and the consultant's organization who together will determine the outcome of the intervention.

Teamwork is fundamental to consulting for a number of reasons. First, a consultant can not rely on authority as the primary method for obtaining cooperation for recommendations or changes. A consultant must rely on the cooperative efforts of individuals. This is especially true in small businesses where the principal contact is most often the business owner. Second, in many consulting situations the implementation of recommended changes will not be accomplished by a single individual or by the consultant. Therefore, the successful implementation of the recommendations depends upon a group or team's motivation to do the work necessary to implement the recommendations. Third, in any consulting situation, the consultant must rely on others to identify and describe key issues from their perspective. Information is the consultant's stock in trade and information will be more accessible in an open, cooperative environment. In short, creating a team atmosphere, fosters successful consulting interventions.

The Building Blocks of Teams

Clarity, Trust, and Responsibility are the building blocks of a high-performing team, and therefore an effective consulting relationship. These factors are represented in Figure 4-1 on the following page; the role that each factor plays in building an effective consulting relationship is examined in the following sections.

Clarity: Value, Methods and Resources

Clarity is a fundamental requirement of any consulting intervention. For several reasons it is even more important to a small business client. First, much more so than for a large corporation, the future of a small business frequently rests squarely on the ability of one, or at most a few individuals, to be clear about strategy, tactics, and resources.

Second, a small business does not generally have the same capacity to check, test, and analyze recommendations that a large business does. Large organizations tend to be inherently more bureaucratic. The benefit of a bureaucracy is that it maintains the status quo, and provides a series of check and balances, a gauntlet, that any change must pass through before being implemented. This series of checks and balances rarely exists in a small business. A small business must be more focused and more clear about the outcomes (i.e., value), the methods, and the resources required for any project or activity.

Third, a small business must act much more quickly than a large business since a small business does not have the resource cushion of a large business. If time is money in a large business, it is much more so to a small business. A small business simply cannot afford to take a great deal of time in making changes.

Thus, creating clarity is the essence of an effective consulting intervention with a small business. It is imperative that clarity be obtained with regard to: (1) the *value* to be created, (2) the *methods* to be used, and (3) the *resources* to be consumed in creating that value.

Figure 4-1: Team-Building and Management Consulting

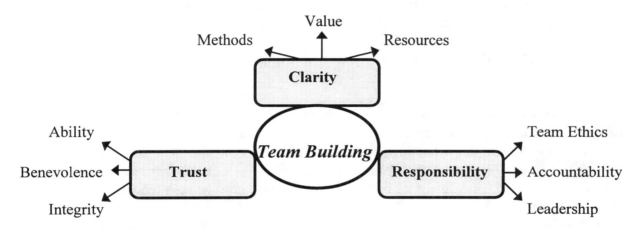

Clarity of Value. To create an effective team relationship between client and consultant, it is important to establish a clear idea of what is valuable to the client. The consultant must know and be able to articulate how his/her participation benefits the client organization. The consultant's value can be examined by answering a few simple but significant questions:

- ♦ What benefit does the client receive from the consultant's work?
    - ◊ What will the consultant do for the client?
    - ◊ What will the consultant do that is unique?
    - ◊ What will the consultant do especially well?
- ♦ What benefit does the consultant receive from this work?
- ♦ What benefit do those who cooperate in this endeavor receive from their participation?

The consultant gains clarity of value by, first, articulating the answers to these questions; answers should be specific, concrete, precise, concise and in writing.

A second way to gain clarity of value is by *listening carefully* to the client's expression of her/his needs. There is no substitute for asking the right questions and listening carefully to the answer. There is an old adage that suggests that 98% of creativity is contained in the question asked and 2% is in the answer provided. Therefore, the consultant must think carefully about the questions asked and listen carefully to the client's questions and answers. The consultant should apply all of their active listening skills here, including:

- *Focus* on the client,
- *Mirror* the discussion, that is, confirm the accuracy of what you have heard by paraphrasing the discussion and asking the client if you are correct,
- *Acknowledge and empathize*, it is important that the consultant understands the client's rationale and feelings behind the expressed needs or desires,
- *Ask* if there is anything more that the client would like to say.

Another way to increase clarity of value is to find and focus on the root cause(s) of the client's issues rather than treating the symptoms (a topic covered in more detail in chapter five). By learning what must be done to create the outcomes that the client wants, the consultant can begin to discover the root cause(s) of the client's issue(s). The client may be clear about what outcomes he/she wants but not know what is required to create those outcomes. For example, a consultant was retained by a consumer products company in Mexico to implement a sales incentive system. The identified issue, the symptom, was the lack of growth in revenue and market share. A consultant was engaged to implement a sales incentive system to increase the motivation in the sales force. The project was thoroughly analyzed and resources were allocated to complete the task. It took nine months to create and implement the incentive system. Everyone working on the project assured the consultant that all was in order. One year later the system failed because free promotional cases given to customers were not reported by the salesmen. The free cases were not subtracted from revenue, and higher bonuses were paid out than were warranted.

In this example, the inadequacy of the accounting controls allowed a major improvement in sales incentive to get off to a rocky start because team members did not acknowledge that the critical supporting factors needed for an effective incentive program were not in place. The rush of time, and the desire to "get on with the new system" contributed to the team's inability to deal with a major problem that would delay implementation. The pressure to complete the work did not allow the team to focus on this issue even though it was brought to their attention by the consultant. The root cause of the issue was the absence of a comprehensive strategy that would improve the support systems needed for growth. Sales incentives and quick fixes to the reward system were not enough to provide the support.

Clarity of Methods.   In addition to clarity of value, it is important for the consultant to establish clarity with regard to the methods or approach that will be used to achieve the project results. Clarity of methods increases the client's confidence that the consultant knows how to successfully complete the project. It also allows the client and consultant to anticipate any issues that might arise during the project. For example, the consultant may be planning to do a market research survey which could prematurely communicate a brand position or promotion dates to a competitor. If the methods are clear to both the client and the consultant during the planning phase of a consulting intervention, then this issue will more likely be identified before any damage is done.

By gaining clarity about how the work will be carried out, the consultant will be able to articulate, with a degree of specificity that is practical, the nature and scope of the work to be done. The Approach and Work Plan sections of the consulting proposal should unambiguously state the methodology to be used during the project.

Clarity of Resources. Clarity about resources is important in two areas: (1) the resources that will be consumed during the consulting intervention to produce the deliverables promised in the project proposal, and (2) the resources needed to implement the recommendations made. Here the consultant's experience and expertise will be important in uncovering the hidden costs in a project or in implementing recommendations.

Consider an example of the hidden costs of a small computer sales and service company. Over the years, the company added products to its product lines without considering the hidden costs associated with the line extensions, including sales and technician training expenses. These costs, though not acknowledged, were real, and eventually served to reduce the perceived knowledge and effectiveness of sales and service personnel. Clarifying the resource commitment necessary to perform the work (in this case, product line extensions) is a valuable contribution that a consultant can make to a small business.

A dramatic example that demonstrates the impact of hidden costs in implementing recommendations involves a well-known Fortune 500 company that engaged a consultant to help them develop a strategy for growth in the 1990s. The consultant recommended that the company pursue a strategy to globalize their business. The company moved aggressively toward this objective, buying out many of their international joint venture partners, and integrating operations on a global basis. While extolling the virtues of standardization in the manufacturing processes as a major strategic advantage, they aggressively added to their production capacity by installing new machines every nine months. Implementation of this plan proceeded rapidly until the first interest payment on debt came due. The company could not generate revenue as fast as they were spending money, and their debt soared to unacceptable levels. The management team was replaced, and the new executive team liquidated many of the company's assets to pay off the debt and merge the remaining business with another Fortune 500 company.

The company did not survive. The hidden cost that they did not adequately consider in their planning was the time value of money. Table 4-1 on the next page demonstrates the point. A four year delay in cash flows turns a very acceptable project, one that adds to shareholder value (Outcome A), into an unacceptable project (Outcome B), one that reduces shareholder value. For Outcome A, the Net Present Value (NPV) is approximately $40,000 per $100,000 investment. This is an Internal Rate of Return (IRR) 20.2%. Outcome B has a negative NPV and a IRR below the cost of borrowing money.

The table shows that a four year delay in cash flows on an investment of approximately $1 billion was sufficiently large to create a major crisis for the Fortune 500 company. A similar error on a much smaller scale would have a devastating impact on a small business. Clarity about resources is very important.

Table 4-1: Clarity of Resources

	Outcome A	Outcome B
Interest Rate	10.0%	10.0%
Investment	$100,000	$100,000
Present Value	$39,978	($1,512)
IRR	20.2%	9.8%
Total Cash Flow	$125,000	$125,000
Year		
1995	($100,000)	($100,000)
1996	$25,000	$0
1997	$25,000	$0
1998	$25,000	$0
1999	$25,000	$0
2000	$25,000	$25,000
2001	$25,000	$25,000
2002	$25,000	$25,000
2003	$25,000	$25,000
2004	$25,000	$25,000
2005	$0	$25,000
2006	$0	$25,000
2007	$0	$25,000
2008	$0	$25,000

Building Trust: Ability, Benevolence and Integrity

Given the inherent risk involved in many projects undertaken by a small business, a client will give a consultant the opportunity to create value and search for root causes of problems, only after some level of personal and professional trust is established.

Trust, in a consulting relationship, is the willingness of the client to be vulnerable to the actions of the consultant based on the expectation that the consultant will perform a particular action irrespective of the ability of the client to monitor or control the consultant (Mayer, 1995). To simplify this definition, trust is the client's reliance on the character, ability, strength, or truth of the consultant (Webster). How, then, does a consultant build trust with a client? What behaviors build trust?

It may seem obvious that the best way to be seen as trustworthy is to be trustworthy. But Mayer, et al (1995) postulate that the key elements of trust are *ability, benevolence,* and *integrity.* Adapting these concepts to the small business consulting situation we find that the key factors in building trust as a consultant are:

- *Ability* - skills, competencies, and characteristics that give the consultant influence within an area (these were discussed in chapter three).
- *Benevolence* - the extent to which the client believes that the consultant will operate in the best interests of the client.
- *Integrity* - the client's perception that the consultant will act in accordance with principles that are acceptable to the client (see the consultant's Code of Ethics from chapter three).

The consultant's task then is to demonstrate ability, benevolence, and integrity through his/her actions - past, present and future.

Present Actions. First and foremost, consultants must build trust by their present actions. These actions include classic advice that is more often acknowledged in the breach than conformance, not the least of which is active listening. By listening, the consultant demonstrates a genuine interest in the client, that is, the consultant demonstrates benevolence. The consultant can only "do good" for the client if the client's needs are met. If the consultant listens, then the client can begin to trust that the consultant is there to help. As mentioned above, learning the technique of mirroring, that is, paraphrasing back to the client what you have heard and understood the point to be, is an important active listening skill.

The consultant must communicate honestly and accurately their abilities and expertise. Being careful not to understate their potential contributions, consultants must stay within the limits of those abilities, and not promise what can not be delivered. The consultant's communications are promises about their abilities and benevolence. It is critical that these communications be accurate and clearly understood by the client. The pressure to "sell" will be tempting in this situation, but this pressure must not be allowed to influence the consultant's representations of ability. Since entrepreneurs and small business managers are legendary for their tendency to prefer action over planning, the ability to articulate clear expectations and promises is critical in small business consulting.

Past Actions. Another good way to establish a trusting relationship with the client is to make available information about past trustworthiness. Before meeting the client, the consultant should reflect on instances of trustworthiness - the times the consultant gave her word and kept it, especially when it was uncomfortable. It is not expected that the consultant would tell the client about all these occurrences; it is more important for the consultant to become aware of their "principles in action." With this awareness the consultant can make adjustments in behavior that detract from trust and communicate or reinforce behaviors and attitudes that engender trust.

In a more formal way, the consultant must be prepared to demonstrate their professional reputation by making available examples of professional accomplishments and professional reliability. These could include testimonials from previous clients, awards from past employers, and stories of successful consulting work.

Promises: Future Actions. This one is simple. The consultant must keep his word in order to be seen as trustworthy. This will require the consultant to be clear about the promises made. An implicit promise that is broken can be as damaging to the consultant's reputation as an explicit promise that is broken. The consultant must take extra precautions and be clear about what is going to be done. (This will be emphasized in the Objectives and Key Issues section of the consulting proposal as explained in chapter five). The project proposal is a *contractual promise* to the client and should be managed accordingly.

Something as seemingly insignificant as punctuality is an important indicator of trustworthiness. Even a small breach of a contract communicates the wrong message to the client. When the consultant asks for a consulting engagement, they ask a client to allow them to enter the client's business. A consulting engagement in a small business creates vulnerability and the client needs to know that the consultant can be trusted.

Establishing Responsibility: Team Ethics, Accountability and Leadership

Responsible behavior is the final building block of a high-performing team and an effective consulting relationship. Anyone who has played a team sport knows that individuals who fail to perform the role that they agreed to perform will cause the team to fail. How can a consultant increase the chances that all members of the team, from either the client or consulting organization, will behave responsibly? Team ethical guidelines, leadership and accountability are all part of responsibility in a consulting relationship.

<u>Team Ethics.</u> Chapter three included a discussion of the professional ethics of consulting. The focus was on the interaction between the consultant and client but the discussion also applies to the consultant's own team. As we will see later when examining the stages of group development, groups go through a "norming stage" in which new behavioral standards evolve (Tuckman, 1965). The consultant can improve the probability of creating an effective team if, during this stage, guidelines that promote personal responsibility and accountability are accepted by team members. By establishing these guidelines for behavior, the client and the consultant develop mutual expectations with regard to responsibilities. This tends to be even more important in small businesses than larger organizations since small businesses tend to be less formal in their interactions, providing the opportunity for misunderstandings.

A few "starter ideas" for guidelines that will promote responsible behavior for both the client and the consultant are:

- During initial stages of the project before committing to the details, the client and the consultant can aspire to any reasonable project objectives and methods that they want. This guideline allows for openness during the initial stages of the project which leads to greater creativity when the team is identifying the problem, defining the objectives, and creating the methods or approach to the work to be done.

- Both the client and consultant take personal initiative for expressing their needs and ideas. This guideline is important if ideas are to have an impact and if motivation through participation is to occur. The first step toward action is to express the idea with team members.

- If team members agree to support another's ideas, then the team members are honor bound to maintain that support inside and outside team meetings. However, if the client or consultant learns that they can no longer maintain support as promised, then they can not make a unilateral change. This issue must be processed by the client and consultant before a change is made.

The mere fact that a discussion of these guidelines occurs often raises the issue of responsibility to the surface and results in more responsible behavior among team members in a consulting relationship.

<u>Leadership.</u>   Leadership is another critical factor in establishing responsibility. It is also a complex and often misunderstood concept. The element of leadership that is most relevant to establishing responsibility is the capacity to persist in the face of adversity. The will and the willingness to keep the common goal or objective as a personal and team objective is critical to the success of a consulting intervention. Since small businesses usually cannot form ad hoc committees or project teams dedicated

exclusively or even primarily to project work, many distractions will compete for the time of the project team. This fact makes the ability to focus and persist in the face of adversity and disruption an important factor in small business consulting engagements.

Accountability. Finally, responsibility is promoted by building accountability into the process. Establishing clear time tables and target dates, and building checks and balances into the project is part of the task, along with creating clarity of roles and assignments.

In general, small business consultants will find that successful consulting relationships are built on the pillars of clarity, trust, and responsibility.

Stages of Team Development

As stated throughout this chapter, an effective small business consulting relationship is based on teamwork. An appreciation of the four stages of the team development process - forming, storming, norming, and performing (Tuckman, 1965) - can be helpful in building an effective consulting relationship.

The consultant's principal challenge is to move from the forming stage to the performing stage as quickly and as effectively as possible -- but how is this achieved? How can team performance be sustained when disruptions and distractions occur?

Forming Stage: Gaining Clarity

In the forming stage, the client and consultant concern themselves with orientation, testing, and with establishing relationships (Tuckman, 1965). Courtesy, confusion, caution, and attempts to identify the particular strengths and weaknesses of team members are characteristic of the forming stage. Often there is confusion as the client and the consultant work to determine the extent to which they share values. In this stage, client and consultant begin to build "bonds of similarity"(Dyer, 1987). It is in the forming stage that team members determine what they want, why they are together, what is in it for each of them. It is during this stage the client and consultant begin to develop the clarity of value and trust that is so critical for effective consulting relationships.

Common barriers to effectively and efficiently moving through the forming stage include time pressures, impatience, inability to analyze the situation, lack of trust, and lack of strategy and focus.

Approaches that may be used by the consultant to facilitate the successful completion of this stage include, being clear about time requirements, being efficient in meetings, yet allowing time for team members to explore, to get to know each other and what is important. One sign that time is being wasted is that there is redundancy in work without benefit to even one team member. The consultant can take time to identify objectives and the extent to which these objectives are commonly held. It is also useful to write down the objectives since team members forget and/or change their mind, and the only evidence of prior agreements is the written records. Finally, the consultant can and should reaffirm conclusions made earlier in the project by brief and frequent reminders to team members. This can be done very efficiently in each meeting.

Storming Stage: Building Trust

The storming stage is characterized by conflict, concern, and criticism as the client and consultant begin to deal with their differences. It is during this stage of development that the consultant's trust-generating skills, ability, benevolence, and integrity must come to the fore. Differences in values and understandings must be resolved during the storming stage.

Common barriers to resolving conflict are the inability to listen, the rigidity of mindsets (that is, the inability of a person to appreciate another's point of view), the lack of negotiating skills, and the absence of creativity in resolving conflict, such as applying majority rule at inappropriate times or without sensitivity to the minority point of view.

The most important thing to do during this stage is be aware that conflict is normal and should not be personalized. Reasonable people have different points of view. The consultant must often act to maintain an equilibrium and remind people that emotional reactions are not catastrophic. The consultant may have to provide advice on conflict resolution strategies, including confrontation, compromise, collaboration, and avoidance[*] . Finally, during this stage the consultant should communicate in positive terms to keep team members focused on what they *can* do rather than on what they cannot do.

Norming Stage: Establishing Responsibility

In the norming stage the client and consultant agree on the rules. By the end of this stage, guidelines for team behavior should be written and agreed to, covering such areas as:

- objective setting
- methods of conflict resolution
- decision-making procedures
- establishing accountability
- agenda management, and
- team member priorities

---

[*] For more information on conflict management see Kenneth W. Thomas's "Conflict and Conflict Management", in Marvin D. Dunnette (ed.), *Handbook of Industrial And Organizational Psychology*, 1976, Rand McNally College Publishing Company. This is considered a classic in the field.

It is at this time that the guidelines of behavior are either formally or informally established, the team code of ethics is set and preferably written. Participation of all the team members at this stage is critical.

A common barrier to efficiently and effectively completing this stage is the belief that this will occur naturally and that the team does not have to "waste time" talking about behavior. This is a mistake and often causes a team to fail to move through procedural issues that interfere with working on achieving the team's objectives. In addition, there can be unspoken rules that team members adhere to but do not discuss, and these may prove detrimental to obtaining the desired outcomes.

Performing Stage: Results

The performing stage is the payoff for the client and consultant. It describes that stage of development characterized by an increased sense of responsibility, greater creativity, openness, and greater personal concern. It is at this stage that the client/ consultant relationship matures and team productivity is at its peak. To get to this stage, the following project management skills are needed:

- Plan - write a clear and specific proposal (as described in chapter five)
- Organize - provide structure, timelines, and accountability
- Learn - review progress and use feedback
- Act - put plans into action

Conclusion

In this chapter, the essential similarity of team-building and effective small business consulting was discussed, highlighting the importance of establishing a firm foundation built on clarity, trust, and responsibility. Ways to gain clarity, build trust, and improve the likelihood of responsible behavior in the client - consultant relationship were identified. Finally, the four stages of team development were summarized and linked with the critical factors for effective small business consulting. Appendix two provides additional information and concrete advice for handling practical problems and opportunities in a small group setting.

References

Bellman, Geoffery M. 1990. *The Consultant's Calling: Bringing Who you are to What You Do.* San Francisco, CA: Jossey-Bass.

Dyer, William G. 1987. *Team Building: Issues and Alternatives.* Reading, Mass: Addison-Wesley.

Greenbaum, Thomas L. 1990. *The Consultant's Manual: A Complete Guide to Building a Consulting Business.* New York: John Wiley.

Herman, Stanley M. 1994. *A Force of Ones: Reclaiming Individual Power in a Time of Teams.* San Francisco, CA: Jossey-Bass.

Holtz, Herman. 1988. *How to Succeed As An Independent Consultant.* New York: John Wiley.

Kampmeier, Curt. May 1996. How To Get And Keep More Business Owners. *Journal of Management Consulting,* 21 - 23.

Klein, Howard J. 1977. *Other People's Business: A Primer on Management Consultants.* New York: Mason/Charter.

Mayer, Roger C. James Davis & David Schoorman. 1995. An Integration Model of Organization Trust, *Academy of Management Review.* Vol. 20, No. 3, 709 – 734.

Schein, Edgar H. 1988. *Process Consultation.* Reading, Mass: Addison-Wesley.

Shenson, Howard L. 1990. *How to Select and Manage Consultants: A Guide to Getting What You Pay For.* Lexington, Mass: Lexington Books.

Shenson, Howard L. 1990. *Shenson on Consulting: Success Strategies form the Consultant's Consultant.* New York: Wiley in Association with University Associates.

Thomas, Kenneth W. 1976. Conflict and Conflict Management, in Marvin D. Dunnette (ed.), *Handbook of Industrial And Organizational Psychology*, Rand McNally College Publishing Company.

Tuckman, B. W. 1965. Developmental Sequence in Small Groups, Psychological Bulletin. Vol. 63, 384 – 399.

Worchel, Stephen, & Wendy Wood, (eds.) 1992. *Group Process and Productivity* Newbury Park, CA: Sage Publications.

Chapter 5

Project Management
for Small Business Consulting

The small business consultant's ability to manage the stages of the consulting *process* is critical to the success of the entire consulting encounter. The purpose of chapter 5 is to discuss the stages of small business consulting and the concept of project management. The importance of a systematic approach to the project is emphasized, and key steps or stages of the process are identified and explained. Particular emphasis is given to two crucial components of the process - problem diagnosis and project proposal writing. Accordingly, guidelines for writing a clear, focused and compelling project proposal are provided, and samples of proposals are included. Finally, we offer appendix one for readers who want to know more about project management software packages available for the small business consultant.

A *project* is a one-time task to be completed within a specified time period. Projects are characterized by a clearly defined objective or scope of work to be performed, a predefined budget, and typically, a temporary organization that is dismantled after the completion of the project (Lewis, 1991). Projects are successful to the extent they are completed on schedule, within budget, and to performance requirements. These three criteria of performance, dollars and time are known as the PDT objectives (Lewis, 1991). *Project Management* is a practical and systematic approach to planning, organizing, implementing and controlling activities to achieve the PDT goals.

The Stages of Small Business Consulting

Consulting projects typically move through a series of predictable stages of development during their life cycle. Many authors and consulting firms have developed their own frameworks to classify these stages. These tend to be very similar in their content as well as in their orientation towards large corporate clients. A review of the literature did not reveal any perspective on the stages of *small business* consulting. We attempt to address this need by creating our own classification scheme, which we call the EPIC Approach, designed particularly for the small business client.

Table 5-1 outlines the four stages of the small business consulting process based on the EPIC Approach - *Exploration, Preparation, Implementation,* and *Conclusion.* This approach is based primarily on our own experience of the small business consulting process and secondarily on a framework offered by Lamar Bordelon, President and CEO of Pound International, Inc. (Bordelon, 1995).

Table 5-1 **Stages of a Small Business Consulting Project (EPIC)**

Project Stage	Project Step
Exploration	Establish Consulting Need Assess Four Types of Feasibility Agree to Develop Proposal
Preparation	Consultant/Client Team-Building Client Review/ Situation Analysis Problem or Need Diagnosis Confirmation of Expectations Delivery Method Determination Proposal Development Documentation
Implementation	Proposal Execution Monitoring Results/ Evaluation Plan Adjustment and Management Reporting
Conclusion	Change Management Final Deliverable Presentation Post-Project Audit

Managing the Stages of the Project

The four stages of the process in Table 5-1 will generally follow one another in sequence. *Within stages, however, specific steps or phases are not necessarily sequential as the table might suggest.* For example, the first steps of the Preparation Stage may be to confirm expectations and then to develop a project proposal. Depending on the nature of the project, the consultant may not wish to proceed to any other steps of the Preparation Stage until after the proposal has been finalized and accepted by the client.

In addition, not all steps will be performed in a given consultation. Again, the specifics of the project will determine whether a particular task is necessary. Especially in a small business consultation, the client may assume responsibility for one or more of the steps of the process. This approach to "chunking" the project is described in the Delivery Method Determination section of the chapter under the topics of to-do list planning and phasing.

The length of each stage of the process depends on the complexity and size of the project, and phases within each stage interact, and may be repeated as often as necessary to complete the stage satisfactorily. Thus, the process may be seen as more iterative than sequential, requiring previously completed stages to be repeated because of the results of subsequent stages (Bordelon, 1995). Each engagement is unique. Keep in mind, therefore, that Table 5-1 is not meant to be a blueprint to be rigidly followed for all small business consultations but rather a general framework for guiding the consultant through the predictable stages and common steps of a consultation.

Stage One: Exploration

The purpose of the preliminary stage is exploration - to determine if there is a "fit" between the small business client's needs and the services offered by the consultant. The client's role is to clearly express the needs of the company and to assess the potential of a consulting intervention. The consultant's role is to understand the client's needs and establish his/her own interest in the project and, if interested, to establish credibility for successfully completing the project. The phases of the first stage are:

Establish Consulting Need. Someone in the small business, usually the owner or a senior manager, must decide that the services of a consultant are needed. As previously discussed, this may be difficult because of a reluctance among small business owners to engage consultants.

Assess Four Types of Project Feasibility. Once the need is understood, the feasibility of the project must be established. Four types of feasibility may be considered - service, financial, technical, and practical. A *service* fit exists between the client and the consultant when the skills, knowledge, and experience of the consultant match the needs of the client. The project is *financially* feasible when the client and consultant can agree on a budget for the project, including compensation for the consultant's services. At this point in the engagement, realistic assumptions can begin to be formulated about the potential costs and results of a consulting intervention.

Beyond service and financial feasibility, however, the project must also be technically and practically feasible. A financial justification can show why a project would be economically desirable to perform, "but if a project is justified on a financial basis alone, the client (or the consultant) may well ignore the technical or practical obstacles which can prevent the project from ever having a favorable outcome" (Bordelon, p 15-6). *Practical* feasibility exists when the intervention can be completed within the time frame of the client, with available information sources, without becoming mired in the quicksand of organizational politics, etc. *Technical* feasibility suggests that the client has or intends to develop or acquire the technical sophistication necessary to accept and successfully implement possible recommendations from the client.

The *MTS technique*, developed by William L. Reeb (1993), of Winters, Winters, and Reeb, is a useful process that can assist the small business consultant in determining overall project feasibility and desirability. *MTS* classifies client resources into three categories: money, time, and skill. Project priorities are set based on the scarcity of these resources. The process works by discretely determining the answers to the following questions during the Exploration Stage:

- Does the client have the discretionary funds to hire outside assistance for this project?
- What is the client's time frame for project completion?
- Does the client have the in-house expertise or skills to perform this project?
- Is the completion time more or less urgent than the need to minimize project expense?
- Does the client have people available to work on the project? Do they possess the necessary skills? If not, can the work be broken down in such a manner that these resources can be used?

The answers to these questions enable the consultant to determine which client resources are available and not available for the consulting project. For small business clients, money tends to be most scarce, followed in order by skills and time (Reeb, 1993). The small business consultant is advised to use this information in planning the project's delivery method and in writing the proposal.

Agreement to Develop Project Proposal. The Exploration Stage is completed when the consultant and client agree to proceed based on an preliminary assessment that the project is both feasible and desirable. At this point the consultant would typically agree to create a detailed written project proposal or plan that will formalize the client-consultant relationship.

Stage Two: Preparation

Once the project has been deemed to pass the feasibility and desirability tests, we move to stage two. The purpose of stage two, Preparation, is to establish productive working relationships with the client, to build a solid overall foundation for the consulting project, and to plan for the execution of the project. The consultant performs an internal study of the small business to define the project expectations and begin the formulation of the project proposal. The phases of this stage are:

Consultant/Client Team-Building. We have consistently emphasized the importance of the consulting relationship in the small business context. This topic was covered in depth in the previous chapter. Suffice to say here that the small business client needs to feel trust and respect for the consultant and is more likely to want to establish a long-term relationship with a consultant who can provide assistance on an ongoing basis.

The consultant and the small business owner should work together to select the team members for the consulting project. Team members from the client organization should include key employees whose leadership and support are necessary for the success of the project. "Gatekeepers" are conduits to information, internal contacts who can provide the consultant with access to needed data, records and people, and are also important team members. In general, employees who are familiar with "how things get done" in the organization are invaluable resources for the team.

Client Review/Situation Analysis. Through a review of appropriate internal records and a series of interviews with employees of the small business, the consultant and his/her team begin to compile information about the client organization. To facilitate this step, consider the following questions and guidelines:

- Does the client have an organizational chart? If so, obtain a copy.
- Who is your client (an individual such as the CEO, a group of senior managers, the entire organization, etc.)? Who will ultimately judge the success of the project?
- Who is your organizational contact (i.e., gatekeeper)? The client and contact may or may not be the same individual.
- Who else in the organization needs to know about your consultation? Who will notify them? How?
- Who do you need to interview to learn more about the organization's culture and the specific problem or opportunity at hand?
- Do different individuals share a common view of the consulting problem or issue? Test the validity of the initial problem definition.

In a project dealing with strategic questions, this step entails conducting an internal situation analysis; that is, to begin to assess the current strengths and weaknesses of the client organization. This includes understanding the culture of the organization, norms of behavior, how decisions are made, and organizational values, as well as the financial condition and resource capabilities of the firm. This internal review helps the consultant uncover the needs or problems of the client in the next step of the process.

Problem Diagnosis. In chapter three, we discussed the qualities of effective small business consultants. One key attribute stressed was the ability to solve problems. This skill requires, among other characteristics, the ability to diagnose problems and needs with accuracy and perspective. In many small business consultations, an accurate pinpointing of problems is the most critical step of the process. Once problems are surfaced and seen for what they truly are, solutions are often self-evident.

It is possible to learn and develop skills in problem diagnosis. An important first step in the process is to identify the organizational level(s) at which the problem exists. Rashford and Coghlan (1994), employing a systems perspective, have developed a useful diagnostic tool for this purpose based on four organizational levels - individual, team, interdepartmental group, and organization. While the four levels of an organization are implicitly linked, problems can often be diagnosed as originating in one of the levels and producing effects in other levels. Table 5-2 identifies tasks at each of the levels from two different perspectives - management and an individual employee. Diagnosing problems by organizational levels can help the consultant to isolate the causes and effects of problems and to provide guidance in the choice of consulting interventions.

Table 5-2: Diagnosing Problems by Organizational Levels

Level	Tasks: Individual Perspective	Tasks: Management Perspective
Individual	Membership and participation	Involving and contributing
Team	Creating effective working relationships	Productive team functioning
Interdepartmental	Coordinating joint effort	Coordination of effective output
Organizational	Adapting to change	Building competitive advantage

Source: Rashford and Coghlan, 1994, pp 14 - 15.

Greiner and Metzger (1983) provide additional insights into problem diagnosis. They stress the need to suspend premature judgment on problems and solutions, distinguish between problems and symptoms, the principle of multicausality, and the interrelationship between causal factors. Table 5-3 summarizes these principles of problem diagnosis.

Table 5-3: Principles of Problem Diagnosis

Principle	Explanation
Suspend judgment	Bring fresh insight and objectivity to the situation. The client's perception of the problem is important but may not be accurate - test the validity of the client's problem definition.
Problem versus symptom	Problems are root causes of situations. Symptoms are the consequences of the problem. Employee turnover and declining market share are symptoms - what is their cause? Ask the question - Why?
Multicausality	Many situations are caused by a confluence of factors, not a single factor. Look for all contributing factors. Ask what else may explain the problem. Be thorough.
Interrelationship	Consider the chain of events that may explain the problem. Perhaps the problem surfaces only when A causes B which, in turn, creates the problem.

Source: Greiner and Metzger, 1983.

Kepner-Tregoe, Inc., (KT) a worldwide management consulting firm that specializes in teaching problem-solving and decision making techniques, offers a systematic, rational approach to problem analysis. The questions that structure the KT process (Kepner and Tregoe, 1981) are:

- **Deviation** - What should be happening? What actually is happening?
- **Specification** along four dimensions -
    - *Identity* - What is it we are trying to explain?
    - *Location* - Where do we observe it?
    - *Timing* - When does it occur?
    - *Magnitude* - How serious or extensive is it?
- **Extraction** of possible causes - What are possible reasons for the problem?
- **Testing** - What possible cause best explains the specified problem?
- **Verification** - How can the true cause be confirmed?

Case in Point. To practice the application of some of these principles and techniques of problem solving, read the following case and answer the questions that follow. What steps would you take if you were the consultant in the case?

A consultant was retained by the general manager of a small manufacturing company. The company had recently installed new robotics and a simplified work system. The changes were expected to increase productivity and manufacturing flexibility, and bring the company into a position of being a state of the art manufacturer in the industry. Instead, measures of quality and productivity have declined, employee turnover has increased, and morale seems to be faltering.

Preliminary analysis by the consultant suggests that the system is fully functional and capable of operating at peak efficiency. Representatives from the supplier of the new system have tested it and reported no problems. Very similar systems have also been successfully adopted by companies in other industries. Interviews with production managers and employees who use the new system have yielded interesting but inconsistent findings. Some feel that the system is inappropriate for the company - "it doesn't fit our needs". Others stress inadequate training provided by the company or a lack of time to realize the benefits of the new approach - " a learning curve issue". Others are strongly opposed to the system but do not articulate a clear reason for their position.

Questions to Consider in Problem Diagnosis:

- Our objective is to accurately define the problem and its causes. Are we prepared to do so given the available information? If we should suspend judgment, what needs to be done to accurately define the problem?
- What are the symptoms of the problem?
- Deviation - What should be happening? What actually is happening?
- Specification along four dimensions -
    Identity - What is it we are trying to explain?
    Location - Where do we observe it? At what organizational levels do we see evidence of the problem? Is there a single organization level that accounts for the origin of the problem?
    Timing - When does it occur?
    Magnitude - How serious or extensive is it?
- Extraction of possible causes - What are possible reasons for the problem?
- Testing - What possible cause best explains the specified problem?
- Verification - How can the true cause be confirmed?

Confirmation of Expectations. After identifying problems and gathering relevant information about the company, the consultant is ready for a reality check on the project. At this point the consultant should be able to accurately, clearly, and thoroughly define the expectations of the consulting project which may then be presented to the project team and small business client. If expectations are mutually agreed upon, the consultant proceeds to the next stage. If not, further client/consultant dialogue is needed before a formal proposal is finalized. When further discussion fails to clear up differences in expectations, this should be seen as an early warning signal and the viability of the project should be carefully reevaluated.

Delivery Method Determination. Assuming expectations are mutually shared, the consultant can begin to finalize a proposal for the consulting project. This proposal will serve not only as a legal contract between the consultant and client, it will become the project plan that will be the primary tool that guides the project to a successful completion.

Since money is a scarce resource in the small business arena, traditional methods of service delivery by consultants are not always feasible for the small business client. Traditional methods typically involve the client paying for a "beginning to end" consultation; that is, the consultant manages all stages and components of the process from start to finish. Some small businesses can not afford this luxury, requiring the consultant to develop creative and nontraditional delivery methods to accommodate the needs of the small business client. Two examples of nontraditional delivery approaches are *to-do list planning* and *phasing*.

- *To-Do List Planning.* Consultants spend their time in a series of small planning sessions focused on identifying client objectives. Each objective is broken into a series of tasks that are articulated by the consultant but performed by qualified individuals on the client's staff. The consultant's skill and knowledge is utilized by the client but the consultant's time is minimized, reducing project costs (Reeb, 1993).

- *Phasing.* The concept of phasing "takes larger projects and breaks them into smaller phases, which are distinguished by a clear set of expectations or benefits. This way, the client can begin a project and commit to each step a finite, manageable sum of money. At the end of each phase, it is up to the client to decide if, when and how the next phase will be carried out. The approach allows the client more control, a better grasp of scarce resources and greater understanding of the benefits of continuing into future phases" (Reeb, 1993).

The use of creative delivery methods that meet the needs of the small business client can increase the demand for a consultant's services and enhance client loyalty, and eventually lead to increased revenues for the consultant.

Proposal Development. Upon completion of delivery method determination, the consultant is ready to develop the formal project proposal. An effective project proposal addresses four major areas: objectives, approach, deliverables, and timing and resources.

- Objectives/Key Issues Identification. This section describes *what* will be done. During the course of the project, the consultant will perform specific objectives and tasks, and perhaps request that others perform tasks. The completion of these tasks will produce the project's results or deliverables.
- Approach. This section describes *how* the objectives will be achieved - the methods used to address the objectives. This is where to-do list planning and phasing may be incorporated, if appropriate.
- Deliverables. This section describes the expected outcomes and benefits of the project for the client.
- Timing, Resources and Staffing. This section describes the time needed to complete the tasks and all other phases of the project. Since "time is money" for the small business owner, timing issues in the project are critical. The resources needed to successfully complete the project are defined, including but not limited to the costs associated with the project. Staffing assignments are also identified, including roles of personnel from both the client and consultant organizations.

Documentation. The consultant presents the proposal in the form of a clear and concise written document. As mentioned, it serves as the project plan, the official client-consultant agreement, as well as a legal contract. Table 5-2 further details the sections that should be included in an effective proposal to a small business client. In addition, we include two sample project proposals at the end of this chapter. These samples follow the general outline described in this chapter and presented in Table 5-2.

Table 5-2: Key Sections of an Effective Proposal To a Small Business Client

Section	Description
Introduction and Background	The introduction is typically an opening paragraph that thanks the client for the opportunity to propose on the project. The background defines the relevant business situation leading to the need for the project. Substantial credibility is added through demonstrating familiarity with the client's industry and the needs of the small business client. "Consultant selling" in the form of new perspectives on the challenges facing the small business provides added persuasive value to a potentially reluctant client.
Objectives and Key Issues	The purpose of the project is defined. This is the most important part of the proposal from the standpoint of quality measurement and management of the expectations of the client. This section should be detailed, that is specific, to the extreme practical, so that there is no confusion as to what the client expects the consultant to accomplish. Objectives or key issues clearly define the business problems, opportunities and/or questions that the project must address or resolve. They are the defining factor for the approach section of the proposal.
Approach	The approach defines and explains the consultant's methodology for completing the project (e.g., personal interviews, market research studies, secondary research). It should be written in a manner that allows the client to understand exactly what the consultant plans to do, why the consultant is doing it, and how the results of the steps are to be used.
Deliverables	The anticipated results and benefits of the consulting project are defined, along with a description of how the results will be presented. For example, if a written report and oral presentation are included, these deliverables should be specified here.
Qualifications	A statement of the consultant's qualifications is provided, if appropriate. Value is added by describing the relevant expertise (skills and experience) that the consultant brings to the project.
Timing, Costs, and Staffing	The time schedule of the project is clearly defined, including target completion dates for each phase of the project. All expected project costs are identified with anticipated timing of expenditures. It is also important to define what nonfinancial resources are needed from the client to successfully complete the project (e.g., internal reports, access to employees). Finally, this section defines project leaders, contacts, back ups, etc. and, if appropriate, work teams for project tasks.
Acceptance	A space is provided for the client's signature as an indicator that the proposal has been accepted and the consultant's assignment has officially begun.

Source: Adapted from the Weston Group.

The proposal should be a professional document that is focused, and easy to read and comprehend. Linkages between the objectives, approach, and deliverables sections should be strong and clear. The small business client does not want to be burdened with the task of reading and comprehending a confusing document. Table 5-3 provides guidelines for writing a consulting proposal to a small business client.

Table 5-3 Proposal Writing Guidelines for the Small Business Consultant

Issue	*Explanation*
Client Involvement	Creating an effective proposal and winning the engagement becomes easier if the client is involved throughout the proposal development effort. Forging a relationship with the client and building a consensus around the proposed solution will ease the doubt of a skeptical small business owner and make it easier for him or her to accept the final proposal.
Focus	The consultant must know the small business client and keep him or her in mind throughout the proposal writing process. The consultant must see the document through the eyes of the client.
Length	Proposal documents can vary in length from short letters to complex documents. The length of the proposal to the small business client will depend on the complexity of the project. It should be sufficient in detail to stand on its own, as if there is no opportunity to personally explain the proposal. However, it should not contain so much detail so as to overwhelm the client.
Style	The best proposals follow a specific outline and maintain a consistent style throughout the document. The rules of good grammar should always be followed. Few clients expect a proposal prepared by a prizewinning journalist but they do expect a document that is professional, well-thought-out, clear, and logical.
Graphics	The old adage "A picture is worth a thousand words" also applies in writing proposals. Effective use of graphs, charts, diagrams, and illustrations may set a proposal apart from the competition. However, overdoing it may overwhelm the small business client.

Source: Adapted from *Management Consulting Services, 2nd Edition, pp. 14-10 to 14-12.*

Stage Three: Implementation

After the project proposal has been accepted by the small business owner, the plan moves into the Implementation Stage. In this stage, the consultant's services are delivered to the client through the delivery method outlined in the project plan. Recommendations are moved from paper and put into action. To the owner, this is the most important stage because this is where the action takes place that will improve the performance of the small business. Plans without implementation do not produce results.

During implementation, the following steps occur: proposal execution, monitoring results, management reporting, and plan adjustment.

Proposal Execution. A well-written proposal is often the key to successful project implementation. If the project proposal includes the proper delivery method and if it accurately defines which tasks are to be performed, when they will be performed, and who will perform them, the implementation stage is often a straightforward execution of the project plan. However, even with an effective proposal, major, unanticipated events can and sometimes do occur.

Monitoring Results/ Evaluation. The consultant must monitor and analyze each phase of implementation in the project to ensure that the project is proceeding as planned. The result of each phase will have a direct impact on other phases of the project. It is vital that the consultant constantly monitor results and communicate with others on the project team and in the small business to ensure that results are being properly evaluated.

Plan Adjustment and Management Reporting. It is rare for a consultant to devise a plan that does not need adjustments during the implementation stage. Effective consultants separate themselves from ineffective consultants by their ability to properly adjust their plan. Ideally, the adjustments should affect the tasks but not the project schedule, resource requirements, and/or deliverables as defined in the original proposal. As previously mentioned, the small business owner is mainly concerned with the cost of the project and its results. An effective consultant will adjust his or her plan as needed to improve results without inflating costs to the client.

If adjustments in the project schedule, resources, and/or results are necessary, however, the client must be apprised and in agreement. The consultant must keep the small business client and the project team updated at all times. This will save the consultant the trouble of having to justify any changes at a later point in the project. During this process, effective communication between all parties is vital.

Stage Four: Conclusion

Change can be difficult for organizations, and small businesses are no exception. While some changes are quickly embraced by organizations, others evoke considerable resistance. Therefore, it is a responsibility of the consultant to serve as a change agent for the small business client. The consultant must prepare the company for change and work with the individuals in the company to accept change.

Volumes have been written on the topic of change management and some consulting firms have built their reputations on their expertise in change management. In the following paragraphs we briefly highlight some of the keys aspects of managing change. A fuller coverage of change management may be obtained by referring to some of the sources cited at the end of this chapter.

Change Management. One of the most difficult challenges of dealing with change is that its impact cannot be predicted (Bond, 1995). Change creates uncertainty and takes people out of their comfort zones. This uncertainty may generate fear in individuals and naturally causes resistance to the change. The objective of the consultant in this phase is to assess the company's readiness to realize the change effort and, as a result of that assessment, better prepare the company for the change process.

The change agent/consultant is advised to see change as a process. Lewin's (1947) view, which has become classic in the field, is that change is a three-stage process of *unfreezing* or preparing the organization for change, introducing the *change*, and then *refreezing* the new changes into place.

To unfreeze the small business and better prepare it for change, *communication, sponsorship* (Bond, 1995) and *participation* are needed. If the reasons for change are properly communicated and justified to the employees, the resistance to change will be drastically reduced. Effective communication will eliminate the fear that breeds the uncertainty. Additionally, the consultant must convince the leaders of the small business and the members of the consulting project team to sponsor the change. If the leaders of the company do not promote the changes, then others in the company will refuse to accept them. Participation in the change is one step beyond sponsorship. Here the client is directly involved in deciding the changes and, as a result, feels a stronger sense of ownership in making the changes happen.

Kanter, Stein and Jick (1992) have developed the "ten commandments of change" which are presented in Table 5-4. Essentially, these guidelines for change can be boiled down to communication, sponsorship and participation as described above.

Table 5-4: The Ten Commandments of Change

1. Analyze the organization and its need for change.
2. Create a shared vision and common direction.
3. Separate from the past.
4. Create a sense of urgency.
5. Support a strong leader role.
6. Line up political sponsorship.
7. Craft an implementation plan.
8. Develop enabling structures.
9. Communicate, involve people, and be honest.
10. Reinforce and institutionalize change.

Source: Kanter, Stein and Jick, p 383.

Once the unfreezing stage has been completed and the organization is prepared, the changes may be implemented. If resistance persists, individuals will need ongoing reassurance that the changes are necessary and effective. Communication, sponsorship and participation must be constant.

Final Deliverable Presentation. At some point during the consultation, typically either just before or after the change management step, the consultant often issues a formal written report and/or presentation to the client team. The timing of this report/ presentation will be defined in the project proposal. The content of the report will depend on whether it is intended to explain recommendations prior to their implementation or to summarize the results of the changes that have already been introduced in the change management step. The benefits delivered to the small business should match those promised in the project proposal. Also, the consultant should accept feedback from the small business owner and project team. This will allow the clients to express their positive and negative thoughts concerning the project. The feedback is a useful tool that the consultant can use to improve his or her service.

Post-Project Audit. After the project is complete, the consultant performs a project audit to evaluate his or her own performance during the consultation. By evaluating all phases of the project, the consultant can identify areas where personal improvement is needed. The goal of this stage is learn from each project so that consultant's service is constantly being upgraded and improved.

Conclusion

A critical step of any consultation is careful planning and project management. This chapter describes the stages of the consulting project and offers specific guidelines for project management. Project plans are specified in the consulting proposal which becomes the cornerstone for the entire project. The importance of developing a specific, tight and coherent project proposal cannot be overstated.

Two sample proposals are presented in the following pages. The first proposal was written for a non-profit corporation that needed input regarding its objectives and strategies. The client was interested in a new strategic plan and in learning new processes for developing and managing its strategies. The scope of the second proposal is more modest. The client was a very small social agency that needed public relations assistance, developing a higher profile and level of awareness in the local community. The client was also interested in learning about grant opportunities for additional sources of funds. While the two proposals differ in degree of complexity, they are similar in following the format described in this chapter.

For readers interested in knowing more about specific software packages for project management, we refer you to appendix one. Several types of project management packages are identified and their features are described.

References

Bond, Victor. 1995. Change Management. *Handbook of Management Consulting Services, 2nd Edition.* New York: McGraw-Hill.

Bordelon, Lamar. 1995. Engagement Management Planning. *Handbook of Management Consulting Services, 2nd Edition.* New York: McGraw-Hill.

Greiner, Larry E. and Metzger, Robert O. 1983. *Consulting to Management.* Englewood Cliffs: Prentice Hall.

Jenkins, Charlotte A. 1995. Engagement Documentation and Control. *Handbook of Management Consulting Services, 2nd Edition.* New York: McGraw-Hill.

Kanter, Rosabeth Moss, Barry A. Stein, and Todd D. Jick. 1992. *The Challenge of Organizational Change.* New York: The Free Press.

Kepner, Charles H. and Benjamin B. Tregoe. 1981. *The New Rational Manager.* Princeton, N. J.: Princeton Research Press.

Lewin, Kurt. 1947. Frontiers in Group Dynamics, *Human Relations*, Vol. 1, 5-41.

Lewis, James P. 1991. *Project Planning, Scheduling and Control.* Chicago, IL: Probus Publishing Company.

Kasdan, Ira 1995. The Proposal Process. *Handbook of Management Consulting Services, 2nd Edition.* New York: McGraw-Hill.

Rashford, Nicholas S. and David Coghlan. 1994. *The Dynamics of Organizational Levels: A Change Framework for Managers and Consultants*. Reading, MA: Addison-Wesley.

Reeb, William L. 1993. Can Small Business Consulting Be Profitable, *Journal of Accountancy,* 2, 54-56.

A PROPOSAL TO DEVELOP A STRATEGIC PLAN

for

WGI INSTITUTE

(Source: Debra Berry, Next Dimension and EMBA '97)

INTRODUCTION

Next Dimension Business Group is pleased to offer this consulting proposal to the WGI Institute. It responds to the need expressed by the Executive Director, Clark Cable, for a new *strategic plan* to aid the Institute in forming options and choosing a strategic direction for the next three years.

A strategic plan begins with the statement of purpose, or vision, of an organization -- a statement that explains why the organization exists and what its goals are. Next Dimension Business Group will use the Institute's vision and priorities stemming from the recent Board of Directors meeting as a foundation. The strategic plan will present a *strategy*, consistent with the vision, that describes how the organization will create and sustain a significant advantage in the marketplace.

Next Dimension Business Group is eager to work with the WGI Institute to develop a strategic plan that will represent the optimal match between the Institute's vision, competencies, and financial resources and the future needs of the marketplace. We are confident that our collective skills will allow us to provide an excellent result for the Institute.

This proposal is organized by sections that describe in detail our view of the project:

> Introduction
> Background
> Objectives and Critical Issues
> Approach
> Deliverables
> Next Dimension Business Group's Background
> Cost
> Work Plan
> Consulting Agreement

BACKGROUND

The WGI Institute is a non-profit research and educational organization that is dedicated to providing the perspective and information needed to solve the critical problems facing global society. WGI offers workshops throughout the United States and in over 30 countries around the world. Over 200,000 people have participated in WGI events since 1972. Most of WGI's existing and planned products depend on up-to-date information, innovative computer programming, and interactive communications technology. The challenge facing the Institute is to ensure there is an optimal match between its business thrust, strategy, competencies, and financial resources on one hand, and the future needs of the marketplace and evolving trends of technology on the other.

OBJECTIVES AND CRITICAL ISSUES

The objective of the project is to develop a three-year strategic plan for the WGI Institute. Accomplishing this objective involves a process that entails additional steps or objectives that also must be completed. Thus, the project consists of the following three key objectives:

Objective 1 Define WGI Institute's organizational capabilities and unique competencies

Objective 2 Define the external environment that affects or will affect the WGI Institute

Objective 3 Develop a three-year strategic plan for WGI Institute

To accomplish each objective, Next Dimension will uncover answers to the critical issues that are listed below each objective. Supplementary issues are associated issues the Institute may wish to consider.

OBJECTIVE 1: Define WGI Institute's organizational capabilities and unique competencies

Critical issues are:

- What are the core competencies of the organization?

- What is the current product portfolio?

- With respect to each product:
    - How and where is it offered?
    - What is the measure of performance?
    - How is it currently performing financially?
    - What is the projected revenue stream?
    - What is the cost of delivering it?

- With respect to the sources of funds for the WGI Institute:
    - What are current sources of funds?
    - What percentage of funding is derived from each source?
    - How stable are the current funding sources?
    - What is the potential for new sources of revenue?

- What is the operating income?

- Does the WGI Institute have a sustainable competitive advantage, or can they develop one?

Supplementary issues are:

- By what internal processes does the organization create and deliver products?

- What internal challenges does the organization face in meeting its goals?
    - What technologies are employed by internal staff?
    - What is the level of technological capability?

- How is funding allocated among various products and operations of the WGI Institute?

OBJECTIVE 2: Define the external environment that affects or will affect the WGI Institute

Critical issues are:

- Who are the current consumers for the WGI Institute's products?

- What is the market opportunity for the WGI Institute's product line?
    - Who are potential consumers?
    - What new products or services would be valued?

- Who are competitors for the WGI Institute's products?
    - Who are existing competitors?
    - What are their products?
    - Who are potential competitors?
    - What barriers to entry exist?

Supplementary issues are:

- What is the potential impact of changes in the technology used to deliver WGI Institute's products?

OBJECTIVE 3: Develop a three-year strategic plan for WGI Institute

The critical issue is:

- Taking the internal and external environments into account, what strategy would represent the optimal fit with the vision, opportunities, and challenges facing the WGI Institute?

APPROACH

Next Dimension Business Group will need to work closely with the WGI Institute to accomplish the three key objectives. We envision working with the Executive Director and a designated "core team" of Institute personnel who are familiar with the key processes and financials of the Institute. The objectives will be accomplished in four phases of activity, which are:

Phase 1	Information Gathering
Phase 2	Information Assessment and Identification of Options
Phase 3	Strategy Selection and Development
Phase 4	Strategic Plan Drafting, Submission, and Presentation

PHASE 1: Information Gathering   Mid-November through December

During phase 1, Next Dimension will begin to address objectives 1 and 2 by gathering information necessary to ascertain answers to the critical issues related to the internal capabilities and resources of the WGI Institute and the external environment. Activities during this phase include:

• Obtaining a copy of all pertinent documents and publications of the WGI Institute. This includes vision and mission statements, strategic plans, product plans, annual reports, organization charts, organizational promotional materials, product and program advertising materials, and financial statements and details.

• Consulting selected personnel at WGI Institute to gain their vision of opportunities and challenges that exist, and to obtain data they might have regarding the external marketplace, key competitors and target customers

• Obtaining product-related data from the WGI Institute, including a description of each offering and proposed offering, processes and procedures for creating and delivering each product, method of advertising, geographic dispersion, trends in demand, customer satisfaction measures, and revenue

• Contacting trade associations, conducting a literature search, and utilizing on-line resources to determine additional information about the marketplace and key competitors

• Surveying past and current customers, if deemed necessary and appropriate

PHASE 2: Information Assessment and Identification of Options   January

During the second phase of the project, Next Dimension will complete objectives 1 and 2 and work with the core team to construct the foundation for objective 3. Activities during this phase will include:

• Organizing and analyzing all the information obtained in phase 1

• Defining the WGI Institute's organizational capabilities and unique competencies, including a review of financial resources

• Defining the external environment that affects or will affect the WGI Institute

• Identifying strategic options that reflect the core competencies, strengths, weaknesses, opportunities, and threats identified by the research

PHASE 3: Strategy Selection and Development   February

During the third phase of the project, Next Dimension will work with the core team at WGI Institute to define the optimal strategy for the WGI Institute and develop the details of the strategy. Activities during this phase will include:

• Developing criteria to be used to "rank" the strategic options

- Determining the optimal strategies, based on the criteria

- Identifying key elements of the process by which WGI Institute can implement the proposed strategies and the benchmarks by which success can be measured

PHASE 4: Strategic Plan Drafting, Submission, and Presentation   March - May 2

Next Dimension will complete objective 3 for WGI during the fourth phase of the project, once again working closely with the core team. Activities during this phase will include:

- Creating an outline of the key elements of the strategic plan

- Writing the first draft of the plan

- Modifying the first draft to reflect input from the core team and other decision makers at WGI

- Providing the final draft of the plan to the WGI Institute

- Presenting the plan to the Executive Director and other designated representatives of WGI

DELIVERABLES

Next Dimension Business Group believes that effective communication throughout the project will maximize satisfaction with the final product. With this in mind, we plan to provide monthly progress reports to the Executive Director throughout the course of the project. The proposed format of the progress reports is:

PROGRESS REPORT

Consulting Project for the WGI Institute

Covering the Period _____ to _____

Key activities during the period:

Significant issues, or findings:

Expenditures:

   Current: _____

   To-Date:_____

Status of project Objectives:

   Objective 1:   ❑ In progress   ❑ Complete

   Objective 2:   ❑ In progress   ❑ Complete

   Objective 3:   ❑ In progress   ❑ Complete

Another key deliverable is a draft of the strategic plan, which will be provided approximately three weeks prior to submission of the final plan. The following schedule depicts the deliverables throughout the course of the project.

Deliverable	Delivery Date
Project Proposal Draft	Completed - November 13
Project Proposal	November 27
Progress Reports	mid-December, mid-January, mid-February, mid-March, and mid-April
Strategic Plan Draft	Late March
Strategic Plan	April 18
Strategic Plan Presentation	May 2

COST

Next Dimension Business Group is pleased to offer their services ..... [discussion of fees]. In addition, Next Dimension anticipates incurring out-of-pocket expenses which would be submitted to the Institute's project coordinator for reimbursement. The estimate of these out-of-pocket expenditures appears below.

EXPENDITURES	NOV	DEC	JAN	FEB	MAR	APR	TOTAL
Literature Research obtaining printed copies of reports							
Travel, Lodging, Meals							
Supplies and Copying preparing bound reports							
Administrative Support							
MONTHLY TOTAL	$	$	$	$	$	$	$

CONSULTING AGREEMENT

This Consulting Agreement is between the WGI Institute and the Next Dimension Business Group. The parties agree as follows:

I. Description of Services   (initials)   ☐ ☐

Next Dimension Business Group will provide services as stated in the "Proposal to Develop a Strategic Plan for WGI Institute" dated November 27. WGI Institute will provide information, access to personnel, and other support as stated in the "Proposal to Develop a Strategic Plan for WGI Institute" dated November 27.

II. Confidentiality   (initials)   ☐ ☐

All non-public information collected from or about the WGI Institute will be treated as proprietary and will not be released to anyone. At the conclusion of the project, Next Dimension Business Group will return all non-public information to the WGI Institute, however, the Next Dimension Business Group will retain one copy of the Strategic Plan deliverable. WGI Institute may designate specific items within the Plan as proprietary, and such items will be expurgated from any copy of the Plan that is shown to any other party.

III. Payment   (initials)   ☐ ☐

WGI Institute will reimburse Next Dimension Business Group for receipted out-of-pocket expenses, not to exceed the amount estimated in the "Cost" section of the "Proposal to Develop a Strategic Plan for WGI Institute" dated November 27.

IV. Term/Termination   (initials)   ☐ ☐

This Agreement will automatically terminate upon completion by Next Dimension Business Group of the services described in the "Proposal to Develop a Strategic Plan for WGI Institute" dated November 27.

V. Designated Contact

The designated contacts are:

For WGI Institute _____

For Next Dimension Business Group: _____

VI. Agreement

By initials of each section above, and signatures below, both parties agree to accept the "Proposal to Develop a Strategic Plan for WGI Institute" dated November 27.

WGI INSTITUTE   NEXT DIMENSION BUSINESS GROUP

_____   _____
(Signature)   (Signature)

_____   _____
(Date)   (Date)

CITY LINE CONSULTING COMPANY
(Source: Erin Hungartner and Associates)

Dear Amanda,

To begin, we would like to thank you, your fellow staff members, and the volunteers of Trabeg House for providing us the opportunity to work with you. By providing much-needed assistance to our city's runaway, homeless, and troubled young people, you do a great service for society as a whole. We would like to help you by enabling you to continue this service.

We understand that your being a not-for-profit organization makes for a degree of uncertainty regarding funding. Additionally, much of your funding is designated only for use in program development, leaving unanswered the question of how to cover general operating expenses. This is a question which we hope to help you to answer by means of the project outlined below.

Following are our *objectives* to be accomplished during the course of the project:

♦ To enhance Trabeg House's public relations for the purpose of generating greater funds from existing sources.
♦ To generate awareness among current donors of the financial needs of Trabeg House as a whole, including overhead expenses and operating costs.
♦ To conduct a financial analysis of Trabeg House to determine if you can improve your approach to raising funds.
♦ To research grant opportunities for Trabeg House.

We will accomplish these objectives by means of the following *approach*:

♦ Acquiring and examining the financial statements of Trabeg House.
♦ Researching and contacting similar organizations which are fellow members of the National Network for Youth in order to discover their means of locating and securing sources of funds and grant opportunities.

- Reviewing each of the three donation request letters which are sent to individuals, corporations, and foundations; determining if any revisions or additions to the letters are necessary, and making such changes where needed.
- Conducting library research to identify grant and other funding opportunities.
- Exploring other avenues for Trabeg House to increase local awareness of its operations.

By employing these methods, we will produce for you the following *deliverables*:

- A list of the funding sources for organizations providing programs and services similar to those provided by Trabeg House.
- A brochure-style breakdown of Trabeg House's general operating expenses and current sources of funding to be included with each of the donation request letters.
- Revised versions of each of the donation request letters (provided that revision is deemed necessary).
- Public relations materials and recommendations designed for Trabeg House's use in future endeavors to generate public visibility for its programs.

Our *costs* for providing these services... [discussion of fees and expense reimbursement].

The *timetable* below shows our intended completion dates for the intermediate stages of our work plan:

DATE	WORK TO BE COMPLETED
October 22.	Submit project proposal for review.
By November 1	Meet with clients to present and review the project proposal.
By November 15	Compile the list of other organizations' funding sources.
By November 22	Review the donation request letters and make any needed revisions and/or additions. Complete research of grant and other funding opportunities.
By November 26	Submit a written progress report to apprise clients of the project's status.
By November 30	Produce the brochure and public relations materials for Trabeg House.
Week of December 2	Deliver the final project presentation to Trabeg House's representatives.

We hope that the project outlined above is agreeable to you. We thank you in advance for your cooperation in providing us with any information which would be relevant to our successful completion of the project. Likewise, feel free to contact any member of our team with any questions you may have. We will keep you informed of our progress. Unless you would like for us to revise any portion of this proposal, your signature will indicate your approval and mark the official starting point of our project. We look forward to working with you to ensure that this, your organization's silver anniversary year, is only one of many anniversaries for Trabeg House.

Sincerely,

City Line Consulting Company

Signature of Authorized Trabeg House Representative   Date

"By its very nature, the small business portion of the economy is turbulent and chaotic. Attempts to collect data on this sector are an immense challenge. New and innovative approaches to data collection and sharing are needed."
<u>Source</u>: The Third Millennium: Small Business & Entrepreneurship in the 21st Century, (1995), p 13.

For at least two reasons, consultants have a particularly challenging task in gathering useful, relevant, timely, and accurate information about small businesses. First, the systems for record keeping and reporting of data of many small businesses are typically not as sophisticated as their larger counterparts. As a result, company information may be incomplete, unavailable, inaccurate, or even nonexistent. Second, despite the crucial role of small business organizations in the economy, they are in many cases not included in the statistical data compiled on a given national industry. As a result, collecting information, especially competitive intelligence, for a small business consulting project can be frustrating.

The purpose of this chapter is to present a conceptual framework for systematically collecting information for small business consulting, one of the special client needs identified in chapter two. The primary emphasis of the chapter is to identify and briefly describe key sources of data for the consultant. These include both published sources (in print and electronic form), and field or primary sources of data. The chapter concludes with a case study, demonstrating the use of the proposed framework to conduct a cost/price analysis for a small business client.

The process of information gathering described here and pictured in the conceptual framework of Figure 6-1, as well as the four key sources of data identified, are valid for consultants on a global basis; that is, consultants should find the basic approach applicable regardless of their country of operation. Information resources and availability, however, can be dramatically different across countries. Therefore, the specific approaches taken by the consultant to tap into the four key data sources will need to be adapted to reflect the information conditions existing in a particular country. The examples and approaches described here are especially germane to consultants in North America, since most sources described are U. S.-based. Selected sources of non-U. S. business information are included at the end of the chapter.

The Illusive Ideal of Company-Specific Data

The goal of the data collection process is to gather the information necessary to assist the client in making an *informed business decision*. The ideal is to find *company-specific* competitive data. Given the lack of financial reporting requirements of small businesses and the general turbulence of the small business sectors of national economies, this ideal is a monumental and sometimes insurmountable challenge. The consultant is then faced with the inevitable compromise of using consolidated industry-level data. Consultants familiar with the nuances of small business consulting, however, remain undaunted by the challenge. In fact, while some key information may not be available at the company-level, it probably is available at the industry-level and can be further refined to a level of specificity that allows clients and consultants to achieve their goal of making informed business decisions. Knowing where to find this information and how to refine it to match the client's specific needs (e.g., geographic market, company size, major product categories) is a key to successful small business engagements. The case of the small printing company described at the conclusion of this chapter describes a successful engagement using the proposed approach and based on a combination of company-specific data and refined industry-level data.

A Framework For Gathering Information

Although information is typically more illusive for the small business consultant, establishing and following a systematic approach to the task will help. The framework illustrated in Figure 6-1 is one such approach. Prior to beginning the first step of the framework, the problem and related issues of the project must be articulated as clearly as possible; this typically will have been done in the consulting proposal from which they may be extracted. From this problem statement, step one of the framework will flow - the purpose and goals of the information gathering process. In step two the consultant identifies the types of information needed to address the stated problems. The nature of the problem will determine the types of information needed. For example, if the project involves the analysis of market potential for a new product or the feasibility of launching an existing product in a new market, the consultant would need to gather data on the structure and competitive dynamics of the industry. This chapter will focus on these types of projects where competitive intelligence is needed.

In step three of Figure 6-1, the consultant considers where to find the required information. What sources are available and which of these sources would render the information in an accurate and timely manner? An obvious first choice is to go directly to the client for information. This may yield all or most of the information needed by the consultant and require little or no additional research. Most likely, however, this will not be the case and the consultant will need to know where to turn to acquire additional information.

Figure 6-1. **A Framework for Competitive Information: Small Business Consulting**

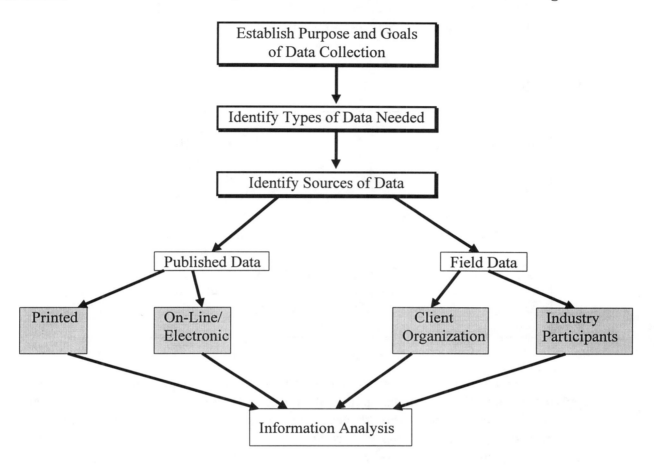

Sources of Information for Small Business Consulting

Assuming the client cannot provide all necessary information (which is often the reason the consultant was hired in the first place), the consultant has three additional options as illustrated in Figure 6-1. First, he or she may turn to sources of data in the field other than the client organization, including industry or company observers. The other options are to review published sources of data, either in printed form or, with the advancement of information technology, to search one of the many databases available.

Gathering Field Data from Industry Participants

In gathering field data it is important to develop a list of possible industry contacts and determine what their predisposition toward cooperation with the consultant is likely to be. Some of the most important sources of information from the field, aside from the client organization itself, are "industry participants" as shown in Figure 1. Industry participants include not only competitors, but firms and individuals in adjacent businesses to the industry (e.g., suppliers), service organizations that have contacts with the industry (including trade associations and consultants) and industry observers (e.g., bankers, regulators). Potential industry contacts are listed in Table 6-1.

Table 6-1. **Sources of Field Data**

Adjacent Businesses	**Industry Observers**
Suppliers	Bankers
Distributors	Auditors
Customers	Regulators
Advertising agencies	Stock brokers
Market Researchers	Industry experts

Service Organizations	
Trade associations	Consultants
Trade conventions	

Not listed in Table 6-1 are competitors who would typically be uncooperative in supplying information given the potential conflict of interest. This does not mean, however, that competitors should never be considered a source of information. Depending on the nature of the project and the competitive dynamics in the client's industry, competitors might be very cooperative in supplying information. Especially in a small business context, some consultants are surprised to find that companies assumed to be competitors may not view themselves in that way if, for example, they each serve a distinctly different geographic market.

Another industry observer that is frequently overlooked is the so-called "industry expert". An index of industry experts is published by *Washington Researchers* and titled "Who Knows What: A Guide to the Experts" (1995).

Service organizations, such as consultants or bankers, are often bound by confidentiality and, as such, are limited in what they may disclose. This should not dissuade the consultant from attempting to conduct interviews or request published reports, however, since these firms can often disclose very significant industry trends or events without revealing confidential information about individual companies.

Of all of the sources listed in Table 6-1, trade associations seem to be an under-appreciated and under-utilized resource of the small business consultant. Trade Associations may be a particularly fruitful source of information, as their mission is to service the needs, particularly information needs, of their members. Many industries have trade associations that serve as clearinghouses for industry data, and some publish detailed industry statistics. Trade associations can be extremely useful in alerting the consultant to any existing published information about the industry, identifying key industry participants, describing and analyzing industry structure, noting important industry trends, and identifying key factors for success. They are also an excellent source of names for field interviews.

Especially among small businesses, it is important to remember that many participants in an industry or observers of it know each other personally. Thus, one source may lead to another if the consultant is adept at his or her task. Particularly receptive subjects for field interviews are often individuals who have been quoted in the media. Another good method to develop interviews is to attend industry conventions to meet people informally and generate contacts.

Finally, the consultant should not restrict his or her analysis to industry participants and observers. Examples of "best practice" are often to be found by benchmarking organizations outside the client's industry and may be easily adapted and transferred to the client. For example, the consultant to a small premium bread bakery studied the Marriott Corporation, winner of the Malcolm Baldridge Award, to determine best practice in customer service and human resource management. Marriott was very cooperative in supplying information and many of their practices were easily adapted and transferred to the client.

Secondary Sources: Gathering Printed Data

Beyond gathering field data from both the client organization and industry contacts, the consultant will need to know how to find information in secondary sources, both printed and on-line. There is a tendency to assume that relevant published data is unavailable for small business clients. This need not be the case and, in fact, for many projects there are a number of very useful sources. The more operative question is not *whether* the information is available but *how* to find it. A good place to begin is to check the guides and materials listed in Table 6-2 on the following page, available in the reference section of most libraries with business holdings. A complete citation for these sources is given at the end of the chapter.

When examining these published sources, the consultant should be on alert for additional sources of information, as published material will often cite industry executives and analysts who make excellent leads for potential field interviews.

Table 6-2. **Guides for Choosing Business Resources**

- *Business Information Desk Reference* - a guide to current print and on-line resources using a question-answer format; contains title and subject indexes, a directory of selected business and trade organizations, and a list of federal departments and agencies that provide business information.

- *Business Information: How to Find It, How to Use It* - a handbook of information describing major business publications and for research on companies, trends, and special topics such as tax law.

- *Encyclopedia of Business Information Sources* - provides a detailed bibliographic listing of business publications by subject and industry.

- *Handbook of Business Information* - provides annotated lists of business publications organized by both type (e.g., index, directory) and major fields of study. Includes a discussion of business research.

The references listed above provide valuable assistance to the consultant in finding *general business* information for the small business consultant. At an industry level, there are other very useful sources. As mentioned above, trade associations are a potential gold mine of information for the small business consultant. To locate a trade association, consult *The Encyclopedia of Associations*, a reference guide which identifies trade associations related to a particular industry and provides information on related publications.

In addition to trade associations, most industries have trade journals which cover industry events on a regular basis. These journals often provide insights for understanding the competitive dynamics and important changes in an industry. Academic and practitioner journals, such as *The Journal of Small Business Management* and the *Journal of Management Consulting*, may also be helpful.

Business researchers and many consultants are familiar with *Dun and Bradstreet's* "Industry Norms and Key Business Ratios" which reports financial norms and industry averages for more than 800 lines of business. These reports, however, are based on the financial performance of large and publicly-traded companies and do not apply to small business. Where can the small business consultant turn to find industry norms for small businesses? *Financial Research Associates* publishes "Financial Studies of the Small Business" which reports industry norms by asset size and sales volume.

Finally, it is always appropriate to consider the information available from government agencies. The Federal Small Business Administration (SBA) provides low-cost and in many cases no-cost services to small businesses, including consultants. *Starting and Operating a Business* is a series published by The Oasis Press which supplies information on the programs and services available from the SBA.

Secondary Sources: Gathering Electronic Data

Advances in information technology are a boon for consultants to small business. Finding information is often only an issue of knowing which of the many databases to search and how to search it. Databases that are among the most useful to the consultant are listed in Table 6-3.

Table 6-3. **Databases/ Electronic Sources for Business Information**

- *DIALOG* - serves as a gateway to more than 400 databases on a variety of subjects, over 200 of which are business-related. DIALOG's Database Catalog contains file descriptions which help the consultant select the appropriate databases.

- *ABI/INFORM* - indexes and abstracts over 800 business and trade journals. This database contains information on companies and products, business conditions and trends, strategies and tactics, and management policies and techniques.

- *COMPACT DISCLOSURE* - provides financial information (e.g., financial statements, 10-Ks, 10-Qs) on over 12,000 publicly held companies; includes management discussion, president's letter, and footnotes to the financials.

- *LEXIS/NEXIS* - provides access to the full text of a wide variety of on-line databases. The LEXIS portion of the database offers legal and regulatory information, while the NEXIS portion is a major source of news and business information, including the full text of hundreds of newspapers and magazines.

- *WILSON BUSINESS ABSTRACTS* - indexes articles published in over 400 business periodicals covering a wide variety of topics as well as specific companies and industries.

DIALOG is a rich resource, providing access to volumes of information. For example, through DIALOG the consultant could access *Dun's Market Identifiers* (DMI) which provides information on more than 7.5 million U.S. companies (both private and public) including current address, product, financial, and marketing information. DIALOG also offers a full range of supporting literature, from individual reference guides for each database to a thorough guide of the DIALOG search system, entitled *Searching DIALOG: The Complete Guide.*

The sources listed in Table 6-3 are particularly helpful in collecting information about factors and trends affecting organizations on an industry-wide basis. Additional databases and on-line resources may be useful for gaining insights on issues affecting small businesses in particular. Two examples are *SBA On-line* and the *Clearinghouse for Strategic Alliances, Trade and Equity Investment*, described below in Table 4. The Clearinghouse is a joint effort of Coopers and Lybrand, Dun and Bradstreet, and the National Business Incubation Association (NBIA); SBA On-line was established by the Small Business Administration (SBA).

The internet contains volumes of data, albeit in a relatively unsystematic format. Literally thousands of small firms have developed home pages on the internet. Finding relevant information may be a hit-and-miss proposition for the small business client, but patience and diligence often reap rewards. Table 6-4 lists just a sample of the information resources available on the web.

Table 6-4. Electronic Resources for Small Business Consulting

- *SBA On-Line* - an electronic bulletin board designed to provide information on topics such as business development, financing services, government contracting, small business facts and programs, and legislation and regulations.

- *The Clearinghouse for Strategic Alliances, Trade and Equity Investment* - an on-line service providing information on strategic partnering. It may assist the consultant or small business owner/manager who is searching for ways to grow a business by locating and evaluating potential strategic partners.

- *SmallbizNet: The Edward Lowe Small Business Network* - a subscription-based clearinghouse for information, representation, and education designed to support entrepreneurs, small business owners, and the organizations that assist them (including consultants), with free and low-cost information.

- *ISO 9000 for Small Manufacturers* - a comprehensive source of information on ISO 9000 quality control standards.

An Example: Conducting An Industry Analysis For a Small Business Client

To illustrate the application of the information framework described in this chapter and pictured in Figure 6-1, consider a consulting project that was recently completed for a small printing company with a regional market (let's call the company, PrintInc.). PrintInc's owner was concerned with his company's declining profitability, and had an inkling that the firm's pricing and cost structure were not in line with competitors. A consultant was retained to investigate the firm's operating expenses and its prices relative to competitors. This project required an industry analysis to obtain the information needed to assess cost and price levels.

Conducting a full-scale industry analysis can be an enormous undertaking; it is complicated when, as in this case, most competitors were regional and private. Given the information resources available, however, it was possible to gather the type and amount of data needed for a precise industry analysis. Following the steps outlined in Figure 6-1 provided a blueprint for a systematic approach to the task of collecting raw data and transforming it into a comprehensive picture of industry structure. In step one of Figure 6-1, the purpose of the engagement was established - to gather the data needed to assess the client's cost and price positions relative to key competitors. Step two involved identifying the types of data needed to achieve this purpose. These data are listed in Table 6-5.

A variety of sources were perused to gather all the data necessary for the analysis. Indeed, each of the sources identified in Figure 1 was needed - printed, on-line, client, and industry participants. One of the first steps was to collect financial information from the client. This was done through meetings and interviews with the appropriate company personnel, including the President, Vice President of Sales, and the Controller. Information from interviews was supplemented by conference calls and facsimile transmissions. PrintInc's financial statements were carefully reviewed and relevant data was extracted for further analysis.

Table 6-5. **Types of Data Needed**

<u>Names of Key Competitors and for each:</u>

Sales Volume	*Operating Income*
Labor Costs	*Income Before Taxes*
Materials Cost	*Number of Employees*
Gross Profit	*Price Quotes by Job Type and Quantity*
Selling, General & Administrative Expenses	

These steps resulted in all the information needed about the client but very little about key competitors and profit leaders in the industry. Given that many of these competitors were privately-held companies, there was some initial concern that the data would be unavailable. This fear proved to be unfounded however, as the remaining sources of Figure 1 were consulted. Information from external sources (i.e., sources other than the client) was obtained using various methods. First, computerized databases such as Lexis/Nexis and ABI Inform were accessed. Searches on these systems were very productive, yielding a large selection of relevant material. For example, several articles from trade journals, especially *Graphics Arts Monthly* and *American Printer*, contained key information on profitability and pricing for the project.

Next, *The Encyclopedia of Associations* was consulted to identify trade associations related to the client's industry - printing. In this case over 40 entries were found under the "graphic arts" heading. For each entry, a contact name and address, telephone number, the year the association was founded, the number of members, publications, conventions/meeting, and other relevant information was typically provided. Three associations proved to be particularly helpful - *Printing Industries of America, Inc.* (PIA), the *National Association of Quick Printers*, and the *National Association of Printers and Lithographers* (NAPL). Interviews with managers from each of the associations were conducted.

These field interviews opened the door to a critical source of financial information - annual financial reports published by one of the trade associations, PIA. Each year PIA conducts a survey of the industry and publishes its results in a detailed financial ratio report for members of the industry. The reports allow individual firms to compare their annual financial performance with that of similar firms. The data are reported by sales volume, product specialty, and geographic area. Two such reports, entitled *Management Ratios: The Printer's Guide to Strategic Management, Productivity and Profits* (one for quick printers and the other for sheet-fed printers [by size and geographic area]), yielded most of the data still needed. After a personal interview with the author of the PIA ratio studies, all remaining cost data were obtained and all data were confirmed.

The final piece of missing data was information on pricing. Providing price quotes to would-be customers is a standard practice in the industry. Thus, a formal request for price quotes on a selection of different job types was given to the client and a small number of relevant competitors, producing all the data needed to perform price comparisons.

Conclusion

Attempts to collect relevant and timely data on small businesses can be a challenge for consultants. The challenge is not insurmountable, however, especially for consultants familiar with advances in information technology. In addition to securing as much information from traditional sources such as the client organization, and published studies and reports, the following steps will help to overcome the challenge: (1) contact industry participants such as suppliers, customers and especially trade associations, and (2) know about the burgeoning sources of electronic information and how to access them for information on small businesses. Advances in information technology can be a boon for consultants who need small business information.

Finally, as previously mentioned, most of the information sources described in this chapter are oriented toward North American companies. To overcome this regional bias, at least partially, we offer Tables 6-6 and 6-7 on the following pages. Table 6-6 lists sources of information on non-U.S. small businesses in print form, and Table 6-7 identifies electronic sources of non-U.S. small business information. Complete references are provided.

Table 6-6: Print Sources Of Information On Non-U.S. Small Businesses.

- *International Business Information: How To Find It, How To Use It* - A timely source of leads on company, marketing, industrial, economic, and financial information for international businesses of all sizes.
[Reference: Pagell, Ruth A. and Michael Halperin. 1994. *International Business Information: How To Find It, How To Use It.* Phoenix, AR: The Oryx Press.]

- *Directory of International Sources of Business Information* - Includes data sources by country and by industry. Data sources include professional and trade associations, banks, stockbrokers, embassies, chambers of commerce and more.
[Reference: Ball, Sarah. 1991. *The Directory of International Sources of Business Information*, 2nd edition. London, England: Pitman Publishing.]

- *The Asia and Japan Business Information Sourcebook* - A guide to about 1000 business information sources, organized by region/country. Sources are presented in categories which include advertising, distribution, industry, management, research and development, etc.
[Reference: Engholm, Christopher. 1994. *The Asia and Japan Business Information Sourcebook.* New York, NY: John Wiley & Sons, Inc.]

- *Encyclopedia of Associations, International Organizations* - Indexes more than 11,000 nonprofit organizations that are international in scope.
[Reference: *Encyclopedia of Associations, International Organizations,* 32nd edition. 1997. Detroit, MI: Gale.]

- *World Guide to Trade Associations* - Contains profiles, including publications, of more than 22,000 trade associations in 150 countries.
[Reference: *World Guide to Trade Associations*, 4th edition. 1995. Munich, Germany: K.G. Saur Verlag GmbH & Co.]

Table 6-7: Electronic Sources Of Information On Non-U.S. Small Businesses.

- *Business and Industry* - an electronic database with facts, figures, industry studies, etc. dealing with both public and private companies at an international level. Coverage concentrates on trade magazines, newsletters, the business press, newspapers, and business dailies.

[Access to *Business and Industry* is provided by two separate information services companies: DIALOG and OCLC, each of which is fee-based. See the web pages for more information: *http://www.dialog.com/* and *http://www.oclc.org/*].

A series of electronic databases on selected regions is available from LEXIS-NEXIS, containing a wide variety of full-text sources of business information. These include ASIAPC - NEXIS, EUROPE Library NEXIS, MDEAFR - Mideast/Africa Library NEXIS, NSAMER - North/South America Library NEXIS. LEXIS-NEXIS is a fee-based information service available through a variety of subscription services. See their web page for more detail:*[http://www.lexis-nexis.com/]*. The ASIAPC source is described below for illustrative purposes:

- *ASIAPC - NEXIS* - an electronic source which contains detailed information about Pacific Rim countries. Covers a broad variety of sources and topics including full-text news from *Asiaweek, Financial Times, Singapore Business Times, Nikkei Weekly*. Also includes business and trade newsletters such as *Asian Economic News, Toshiba Weekly*. [Reference: ***Lexis-Nexis Inc.***, P.O. Box 933, Dayton, Ohio 45401].

References: Print Sources

Encyclopedia of Business Information Sources. 1995/96. Detroit, MI: Gale Research Company.

Financial Studies of the Small Business, 18th edition. 1995. Winter Haven, FL: Financial Research Associates

Freed, Melvin N. 1991. *Business Information Desk Reference: Where to Find Answers To Business Questions.* New York, NY: Macmillan Publishing Co.

Jenkins, Michael D. 1994. *Starting and Operating a Business.* Grants Pass, Oregon: The Oasis Press.

Lavin, Michael R. 1992. *Business Information: How to Find It, How to Use It.* Phoenix, Arizona: The Oryx Press.

Strauss, Diane Wheeler. 1988. *Handbook of Business Information: A Guide for Librarians, Students, and Researchers.* Englewood, Colorado: Libraries Unlimited, Inc.

The Third Millennium: Small Business and Entrepreneurship in the 21st Century. 1995. Office of Advocacy, U.S. Small Business Administration, Washington,   D.C.

Who Knows What: A Guide to the Experts. 1995. Washington, D.C.: Washington Researchers.

Electronic Sources

ABI/INFORM, UMI, P.O. Box 1346, 300 North Zeeb Road, Ann Arbor, Michigan 48106.

Clearinghouse for Strategic Alliances, Trade and Equity Investment. 1995. National Business Incubation Association, Athens, Ohio.

Compact Disclosure, Disclosure Incorporated, 5161 River Road, Bethesda, Maryland 20816.

DIALOG, Knight-Ridder Information Inc., 2440 El Camino Real, Mountain View, California 94040-1400.

Lexis-Nexis Inc., P.O. Box 933, Dayton, Ohio 45401.

Electronic Sources (continued)

Wilson Business Abstracts, H.W. Wilson Company, 950 University Ave. Bronx, New York 10452.

```
┌─────────────────────────────────────────┐
│                                           │
│              Chapter 7                    │
│                                           │
│      Facilitate Strategic Thinking and    │
│        Organizational Learning            │
│                                           │
└─────────────────────────────────────────┘
```

Thus far, we have discussed three of the four special client needs identified in chapter two -- building consulting relationships, project management, and, in the preceding chapter, accessing data, especially competitive information. The fourth special need of the small business client is strategic planning, and especially, creating a sense of "strategic thinking". The purpose of chapter seven is to examine this need.

Strategy consultations are among the most common types of interventions we have provided. Sometimes the projects are relatively simple -- a small bank wants advice on whether and how to expand its lending programs to include student and automobile loans, or a retirement community wants to know the costs and potential of developing an adult day care satellite. These types of strategic questions require market research studies and competitive analyses, more than anything. They ask rather focused questions, such as: should we enter this new market?... offer this new program?... expand or contract our product or service offerings?... what is the size and potential of the market? An implicit strategy (or sometimes explicit one) already exists, and the consultant is hired to analyze the market and offer strategy recommendations.

Other times, the client's questions are more open-ended and typically more urgent. They take the form of: we need help to determine where we're going; we're losing business (or market share, profits, customers, etc.) and we need to do something; we need a sense of purpose and direction. In this scenario, the client often needs (without knowing and articulating it) a sense of "strategic thinking". The difference between a client who wants a market research study or a competitive analysis and one that is searching for a sense of strategy is enormous. While both types of needs are important, the focus of this chapter is on the latter, developing a sense of "strategic thinking" within the small business.*

---

* Consultants interested in tools and techniques for market research or competitive analyses will find many sources available on these topics. For information on market research, for example, see David Aaker's *Strategic Market Management* (New York: John Wiley & Sons, Inc., 1995, chapters 3 & 5). See Michael Porter's *Competitive Strategy* (New York: The Free Press, 1980) for a popular approach to industry analysis.

Developing a sense of strategic thinking is different than developing a strategic plan. Some clients approach us with the idea that they need a strategic plan and we can provide it. Even if this was true and we developed their strategic plan, it too often becomes just another planning document that inevitably ends up collecting dust on the shelf. More important than providing the strategic plan itself, we stress the need to establish a *process* of strategic thinking and planning. After all, is it better to give the proverbial hungry man a fish, or to teach him how to fish? Our preferred approach is to be a catalyst for client learning rather than presuming to be the omniscient consultant. In terms of the types of consulting explained in chapter three, we prefer to deal with strategic consultations from a *process* rather than *content* approach. This approach is summarized in Table 7-1 as the contemporary approach.

Table 7-1: Two Views of Consulting

Traditional View	Contemporary Process View
consultants ...	*consultants ...*
• provide answers	• foster learning
• are industry experts	• are knowledge brokers
• are substitute brains	• are catalysts for change
• make clients dependent	• embed capacity in client organizations

Source: Hamel, 1997.

The purpose of this chapter is to describe a philosophy or style of management that facilitates strategic thinking and organizational learning, one of the critical needs of many small businesses. This approach stresses the importance of process, and rests on the pillars of employee collaboration, organizational innovation and accountability. In addition, at the end of the chapter we offer concrete examples of participative planning designs that are practical applications of the approach we describe. We begin first with an explanation of the premises or assumptions we hold regarding strategic management in small businesses. As we have previously discussed, studies confirm the importance of strategic thinking for small businesses and consistently cite a lack of strategy as one of the leading causes of small business failures. This chapter addresses this deficiency by offering a model and practical advice for small business consulting.

Premises About Strategy

Strategic management is a relatively new and dynamic field of study, and many views, sometimes conflicting views, exist about the topic. The field seems to be in a transitional stage, with new ideas constantly emerging. The late 1980s and early 1990s marked a period of unprecedented downsizing. Companies focused on quality, cost-cutting, and reengineering programs, with mixed results. These efficiency approaches, however, did very little to create growth and generate distinctive competitive advantages. As a result, a new era has dawned with growth and strategy reemerging as "the single most important management issue" according to a study by the Association of Management Consulting Firms (*Business Week*, August 26, 1996).

In light of this renewed focus on strategy, we describe a few practical frameworks for assisting clients with strategic questions. Before doing so, the reader should understand our assumptions about strategy, particularly as it relates to the management of small businesses.

Strategic Thinking is Scarce

According to Hamel and Prahalad (1989), strategic thinking, or "strategic intent" as they call it, is an *active management process* that includes:

focusing the organization's attention on the essence of winning; motivating people by communicating the value of the target; leaving room for individual and team contributions; sustaining enthusiasm by providing new operational definitions as circumstances change; and using (strategic) intent consistently to guide resource allocations. (p 64).

Especially in small organizations, strategic thinking is rare. In chapter two we discussed some of the reasons for this, including the tendency for owner/managers to be preoccupied with day-to-day operations, to be overwhelmed with details (Woodard, 1992), to be short-term focused, and to be pulled in too many different directions by the need to be involved in all aspects of the business. Accordingly, a recent AICPA survey found that the single most important piece of advice from management consultants to small business managers was to use strategic planning. Indeed, this was identified in chapter two as one of the special needs of the small business client.

A related problem with the small organization is that the senior manager may have a very clear idea of strategy in his own mind but lack the mechanisms and/ or training to communicate that strategy. This seems to be particularly true in the social agencies we have consulted. The directors of these institutions rarely have any formal business education. They become directors because of their passion for addressing a social injustice (e.g., hunger, homelessness) and because of their leadership skills. Management skills are learned on-the-job, if at all. We have found many who view strategy as something that is (or should be) simply understood, and management as making sure the agency pays its bills, that is, something that distracts them from their ministry of serving the disadvantaged.

Strategy is also often a problem for the successful entrepreneur who wants to take her business to the next level of success. This seems to be especially true in the case of entrepreneurs who start a business with a great idea, supported by their own energy and vision, but encounter severe problems after clearing an initial hurdle of success. As the business grows and more employees are hired, (i.e., as the business moves from its infancy stage to growth and maturity), ways of communicating the strategy of the founder and infusing the organization with a sense of energy, purpose and commitment are needed. This is a new challenge for a successful entrepreneur, different than the challenge of achieving initial market acceptance for a new product, service or program. The entrepreneur needs new skills and knowledge to be a steward of the "active management process" (Hamel & Prahalad, 1989) needed to build strategic thinking.

Strategy Requires Innovation, Learning

A second premise is that strategic thinking requires innovation, which in turn, depends on organizational learning. The concept of a learning organization has been popularized by several recent authors, most notably Peter Senge, author of *The Fifth Discipline* (1990). According to Harvard Business School professor David Garvin (1993), a learning organization is "an organization skilled at creating, acquiring, and transferring knowledge, and at modifying its behavior to reflect new knowledge and insights" (p 80).

We believe that strategy, now more than ever, requires a dynamic process of generating new ideas, that is, strategy depends on learning and creativity. Traditional models of strategy have been very heavy on analysis and rather light on the importance of creativity (Hamel & Prahalad, 1989). Perhaps there was a time when this relative emphasis was acceptable, even appropriate. But competition in most industries is more dynamic now than it has ever been, and competitive advantage more fleeting. Especially in mature industries, successful new products are quickly imitated by competitors and advantage is temporary. Competitive industries are characterized by "the cycle of innovation - imitation - equilibrium" (Werther & Kerr, 1995), as shown in Figure 7-1.

Figure 7-1: The Cycle of Competitive Imitation

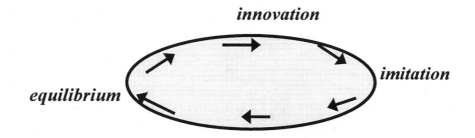

Under these circumstances, characterized by accelerated rates of industry change and rapid diffusion of innovation, Liedtka (1996) argues that "today's product is no more than a temporary solution to today's customer problem -- it offers no hope for sustaining an advantage" and, the ability "to continuously build new capabilities is at the heart of competitive advantage" (p 21). In this case, the essence of advantage focuses on the identification and development of organizational *processes* rather than on particular *products* or *markets,* processes that produce meaningful and continuous learning and strategic innovation in the organization. In short, the ability to develop an ongoing flow of innovation provides a path to competitive advantage in fast-paced environments.

When these conditions do not prevail, that is, when competition is rather staid and industry change is relatively slow, innovation is less critical and the traditional analytical models of strategy would be acceptable. The traditional approach would entail a SWOT analysis, identifying the internal strengths and weaknesses of the organization, along with its external opportunities and threats, and seeking a strategic fit between the two sets of factors. Using this approach, strategic changes tend to be more "incremental", representing marginal adjustments from the status quo. Our bias in this chapter is to stress the innovation/ learning model rather than this more traditional technique.

Learning organizations are skilled at five main activities, according to Garvin (1993, p 81): systematic problem-solving, experimentation with new approaches, learning from their own history and experience, learning from the experience and best practice of others, and transferring knowledge quickly throughout the organization. These activities are built into the planning methods discussed at the end of this chapter. The first activity, systematic problem-solving, is also addressed in chapters five and eight. Each of these activities rests on the need to involve employees in an engaging and meaningful planning process, as described in the next section.

Strategy Requires Collaboration

A third premise of our approach to planning is that strategic thinking requires meaningful participation by diverse stakeholders, including, of course, employees, but also external groups such as suppliers, customers, and even, depending on circumstances, competitors. Regarding employee involvement, Bartlett & Ghoshal (1995) contend that the new role of top management is "to unleash the human spirit, which makes initiative, creativity, and entrepreneurship possible" (p 132). This is achieved by moving away from the top-down, control-oriented model of planning to approaches that nurture the innovative ideas of front-line employees such as sales representatives and engineers, and create a sense of shared purpose. This view is aptly stated in *The Fifth Discipline Fieldbook* (1994):

> Thus, at the heart of building shared vision is the task of designing and evolving ongoing processes in which people at every level of the organization, in every role, can speak from the heart about what really matters to them and be heard - by senior management and each other. The

quality of this process, especially the amount of openness and genuine caring, determines the quality and the power of the results... a true shared vision cannot be dictated; it can only emerge from a coherent process of reflection and conversation (p 299).

The goal of a collaborative planning process is not necessarily 100% participation of all employees. This may be an unrealistic standard for many reasons, including the prohibitive costs, in time and money, of full participation, and the lack of enthusiasm for participation by some employees. Instead, the goal is to create "a hierarchy of imagination" (Hamel, 1997). The conventional view is that strategy is the domain of top management but the hierarchy of imagination concept stresses the importance of including key people from each level of the organization, as shown in Figure 7-2.

Figure 7-2: The Hierarchy of Imagination

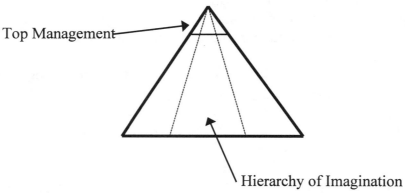

Source: Hamel, 1997.

This inclusive approach to planning brings new voices, new perspectives and new energy to the process. It allows the organization to tap into the knowledge of its people. Gaining this input may be a key to competitive advantage, according to Bartlett & Ghoshal (1995):

In the emerging information age, the critical scarce resource is knowledge... (not capital). The implications for top-level managers are profound. If front-line employees are vital strategic resources instead of mere factors of production, corporate executives can no longer afford to be isolated from the people in their organizations (p 142).

These changes call for a planning process where employees can come together and contribute "through a constant interactive process aimed at consensus" (Bartlett & Ghoshal, 1995, p 142). A technique designed to achieve this collaboration and consensus, the interview approach, is described at the end of the chapter.

Involvement in the planning process can and often should extend beyond the confines of the organization to include key external stakeholders. To keep the process close to the realities of the market:

> strategy should also include interaction with key customers and suppliers. That openness alone marks a revolution in strategic planning, which was always among the most sacrosanct and clandestine of corporate activities. But it's necessary if the process is to produce what customers want (*Business Week*, August 26, 1996, p 48).

Collaborative planning is important for still another reason. As discussed in chapter five, managing change can be a challenge in organizations. Open communication and ongoing participation of employees are two guidelines for overcoming resistance to the change. The foundation of collaborative planning approaches is built on these guidelines, and addresses several of the ten commandments of change described in chapter five (e.g., create a shared vision and common direction, develop enabling structures, communicate, involve people, and be honest).

Strategy Requires Accountability

Our final planning premise is that strategy requires accountability. Two popular notions in management are: (1) if you can't measure it, you can't manage it (Garvin, 1993, p 89), and (2) what you measure is what you get (Kaplan & Norton, 1992, p 71). A classic article in the Organizational Behavior field, Steven Kerr's (1975) *The Folly of Rewarding A, While Hoping for B,* echoes this theme. An organization's measurement and reward system affects the behavior of managers and employees. Put another way, without adapting the reward system to accommodate the types of collaborative planning we advocate here, realizing the benefits of the new planning processes is a hit-or-miss proposition. In short, a good planning process is one that measures progress and builds accountability into the organization. A good measurement system is one that fosters the types of behavior that promote strategic thinking.

The problem with the traditional approach to measuring corporate performance is its narrow focus on financial measures like return-on-investment and earnings-per-share. These measures, according to Kaplan & Norton (1992), "can give misleading signals for continuos improvement and innovation--activities today's competitive environment demands. The traditional financial measures worked well for the industrial era, but they are out of step with the skills and competencies companies are trying to master today" (p 71).

In place of strictly financial measures, Kaplan & Norton suggest a "balanced scorecard". This approach allows managers to assess performance in several areas simultaneously, a requirement for managing in an increasingly complex and competitive era. Specifically, the balanced scorecard looks at performance from four perspectives -- financial, customer, operations, innovation, as shown in Figure 7-3. This model can be adopted by small businesses and tailored to fit the particular goals, constraints and circumstances of the organization. Adapting the Kaplan & Norton model, we suggest that the following types of questions be asked to assess the performance of the small business planning process:

- How are we doing *financially*? (measures of growth, profitability, cash flow).
- How do *customers* [or patients, students, clients, parishioners, etc.] see us? (measures of customer satisfaction, customer service, number of new customers, quality, on-time delivery).
- How are we doing with *operations* and *employees*? (measures of employee satisfaction, productivity and efficiency, cycle time, response time).
- Continuous *learning* and improvement - Are we creating new ways to succeed? (measures of the number and success of new product or process introductions, time needed to introduce innovations).

Figure 7-3: The Balanced Scorecard

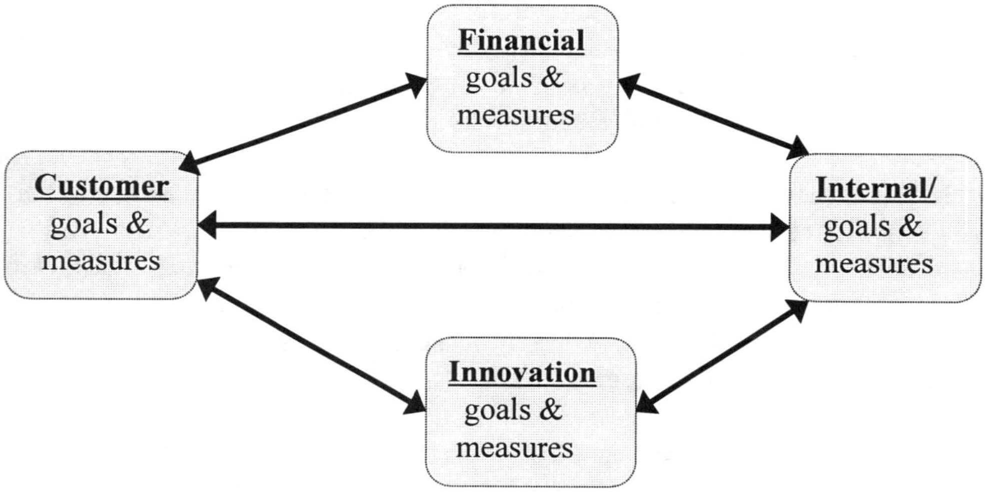

Source: Adapted from Kaplan & Norton, 1992.

Clearly, the precise nature of questions asked and measures adopted will depend on the organization's mission and strategy. The questions above and the model of Figure 7-3 are merely meant to serve as a generic model which will prompt the client organization's own unique questions and ideas. The key point is not the particular questions we have raised but the need to build accountability into the strategy process, an accountability that is designed to promote rather than stifle collaboration, creativity and innovation.

Conclusion

The preceding premises clearly establish the importance of the *process* of planning. Strategic thinking is the outcome of a style of management, it cannot be mandated by top-down management directives. Figure 7-4 summarizes our approach and underscores the importance of process. The goal of strategy is to create value for the customer and competitive advantage for the organization. Value and advantage come from doing different things or doing things differently, which in turn, requires acts of creativity, will and boldness. Acts of innovation and boldness are higher-level human achievements that are the result of employees who are engaged and committed to a purpose. Described at the end of this chapter are just a few examples of field-tested planning methods and designs that seek to achieve innovation and commitment through involving diverse stakeholders in the planning process.

Figure 7-4: **The Importance of Process**

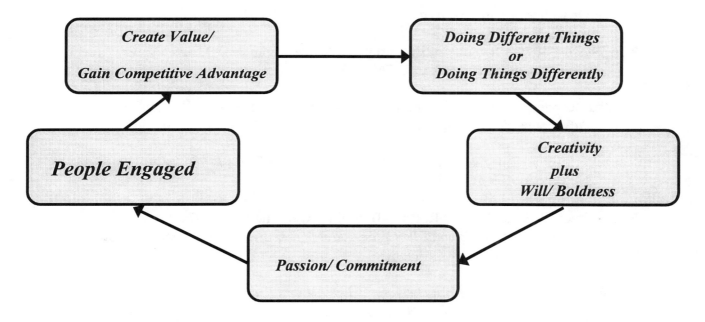

References

Aaker, David A. 1995. *Strategic Market Management.* New York, NY: John Wiley & Sons, Inc.

Bartlett, Christopher A. & Sumantra Ghoshal. May-June 1995. Changing The Role of Top Management: Beyond Systems To People, *Harvard Business Review*, 132 - 142.

Garvin, David A. July-August 1993. Building A Learning Organization, *Harvard Business Review*, 78 - 91.

Hamel, Gary & C. K. Prahalad. May-June 1989. Strategic Intent, *Harvard Business Review*, 63 - 76.

Hamel, Gary. August 1997. Presentation to *The Academy of Management*, Boston, MA.

Kaplan, Robert S. January-February 1992. The Balanced Scorecard - Measures That Drive Performance, *Harvard Business Review*, 72 - 79.

Kerr, Steven. 1975. The Folly of Rewarding A, While Hoping for B, *Academy of Management Journal*, vol. 18, 769 - 783.

Liedtka, Jeanne M. 1996. Collaborating Across Lines of Business for Competitive Advantage, *Academy of Management Executive*, Vol. 10, No. 2, 20 - 34.

Napier, Rod & P. Sanaghan, C. Sidle. 1997. *Tools and Activities for Strategic Planning*, New York: McGraw Hill.

Senge, Peter M. & C. Roberts, R. Ross, B. Smith, A. Kleiner. 1994. *The Fifth Discipline Fieldbook: Strategies and Tools for Building a Learning Organization.* New York, NY: Doubleday/Currency.

Senge, Peter M. 1990. *The Fifth Discipline: The Art and Practice of the Learning Organization.* New York, NY: Doubleday/Currency.

Strategic Planning. August 26, 1996. *Business Week*, 46 - 52.

Weisbord, Marvin. 1992. *Discovering Common Ground.* San Francisco: Berrett-Koehler.

Werther, William B. & Jeffrey L. Kerr. May-June 1995. The Shifting Sands of Competitive Advantage, *Business Horizons,* 11 - 20.

Woodard, Wiley M. 1992. Help Wanted. *Black Enterprise*, 2: 219-222.

*The Future Search Model**

Described below, in outline form, is the *Future Search* model. This approach has been used in many settings with many different types of organizations (business, non-profits, education, health care, etc.). The approach is designed to involve multiple stakeholders, both internal and external to the organization, in the planning process. As described below, the process takes place over two and a half days, although this can be modified to suit the needs and constraints of the client. Weisbord has found that the approach works best with 25 - 60 participants, when the organization is in a period of transition, and when organizational leaders are visible and engaged in the process.

An overview of the process is shown in Figure 7-5 and explained beginning on the following page. Keep in mind that the overview is an outline not a prescription; the specific design of the process will need to be adapted to the client's unique circumstances.

Figure 7-5: **The Future Search Process**

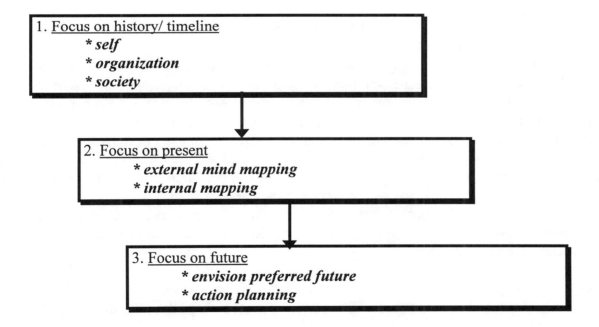

---

* Marvin Weisbord, author of *Discovering Common Ground* (San Francisco: Berrett-Koehler, 1992), describes the practice and pitfalls of "Future Search" conferences. We are indebted to consultants Rod Napier and Pat Sanaghan for introducing us to this, and many other, interactive planning models. Napier and Sanaghan, along with Clint Sidle, have published a book on the topic (*Tools and Activities for Strategic Planning*, New York: McGraw Hill, 1997).

DAY 1 - Afternoon

Focus on the Past - Who We Are, Where We Have Been, How We View World Trends, What We Want For the Future.

Typical Tasks: Three lists written on newsprint and posted on the wall - Self, World, Organization (or Sector, Community, etc. as appropriate).

Each person notes milestones and trends over a given number of years, and records their items on the newsprint. Mixed stakeholder groups analyze the items, and report (1) similarities/ differences/ values, (2) probable and ideal futures (World, Sector). Agreed upon conclusions are noted (look for "common ground").

Purposes of Phase: (1) Promote shared leadership. Every person in the room is writing on flip charts within 45 minutes of the start, thus making real that all have contributions to make. All flip charts remain on the walls throughout. (2) Build community quickly (people appreciate facts of each others' lives, recognize common needs, etc.) (3) Establish global context for local issues (e.g. "Think globally, act locally).

DAY 2 - Morning

Focus on the Present - External: - We make a group "mind map" of world trends as they affect the organization/issue being studied (e.g., we ask the question: What external factors are affecting our organization's ability to achieve excellence?). Each person indicates on the map his/her own priorities. Then, stakeholder groups (i.e., groups with common interests or roles) each analyze the map for (1) important priorities to us, (2) what we (i.e., the organization) is doing now, and (3) what we need to do in the future. All groups report, and similarities and differences in perception are noted and discussed.

Purposes of Phase: - (1) Discover impact of current world trends on stakeholders, how each group is responding, and what they want for the future; (2) Establish future priorities and discern interdependencies.

Focus on the Present - Internal: - Each stakeholder group lists current "prouds" (i.e., what we feel good about) and "sorries" (i.e., recent regrets) regarding the organization. They indicate which they want to continue, drop, or enhance in the future. Lists are posted and discussed.

Purposes of Phase: - (1) Discover values (what's important) for each group; (2) Discern "current reality" -- our perceived pluses and minuses.

DAY 2 - Afternoon

Focus on the Future: - Mixed stakeholder groups imagine ideal future scenarios. They travel into the future and choose a way of dramatizing what they find (e.g., a 60 Minutes segment, or a play, or a <u>Fortune</u> cover story that features their organization and its accomplishments). They report concrete details as if they have already happened or are happening right now. They build in values, practices, policies derived from earlier phases.

Volunteers observe common and unique features of all scenarios and present for group discussion/validation.

<u>Purposes of Phase:</u> - (1) Provide value-based, hopeful foundation for immediate action planning. Discover what people <u>really</u> want to spend their time on now ("Today is yesterday's future.") - (2) Think systemically about the whole, rather than the problems; (3) Engage in purposeful dialogue across all boundaries.

DAY 3 - Morning

A Consensus Scenario: - Common features are highlighted and validated by the whole group. Groups are asked to consider which unique features they would like to incorporate into the common scenario. This document becomes the ideal "preferred future."

<u>Action Planning:</u> - Volunteers, or stakeholder groups, make long and short range action plans to start implementing the ideal strategic future. Their plans are reported to the conference before closing, and plans are made for collecting and disseminating the learning and documents.

<u>Purpose:</u> - To act together now on whatever common ground has been discovered toward the ideal futures.

The Interview Design*

Well-designed activities can increase the participation of people within a large group setting and can increase the quality of the information generated. Following is a large group intervention used with 65 managers and their bosses, who represented the

---

* We were first introduced to this data-gathering technique by consultants Rod Napier and Pat Sanaghan. This description comes from Napier & Gershenfeld, *Groups: Theory and Experience, 5th edition* (1993, Houghton Mifflin Company). Thanks to Rod Napier and Pat Sanaghan for encouraging the use of this description.

strategic planning committee of an organization of 3,000 employees. The interview design described here offered a broad spectrum of middle managers an opportunity to influence the ultimate planning process of their organization.

- Prior to the day-long meeting, individuals were requested to submit questions they believed the group should address at the outset of any strategic planning process. The questions could be general or as specific as desired. With the help of a consultant, a small, representative group selected the six most powerful and useful questions that they believed the total group of managers needed to address.

- Upon entering the session, the 72 leaders were requested to take a chair in any of the rows. What they saw were six groups of twelve chairs, each consisting of six chairs facing six chairs (see Figure 7-6). On each chair was a typed question, a note pad, and a pencil. The leaders were told that there were six different questions in their row and the same six questions in each of the rows in the room, although the rows were arranged so that a person with a different question was across from them.

When the design began, the people in Row A asked the people across from them in Row B their question. They were to probe with follow-up questions, attempting to gain as much information as possible. Seeking examples was essential. Each had approximately three minutes to do this and record their responses. A timer called time at the end of three minutes, at which point the individual across from the first interviewer had an opportunity to ask his or her question. Again, individuals had three minutes to respond. At the end of the allotted time, the round ended with all the individuals in both rows having answered a question and having asked a question. Now the people in Row A were asked to move one seat to their right (the first person rotated to the rear; see figure below). The people in Row B remained stationary. Thus each individual had another person to interview on her or his question and had the opportunity to be interviewed on another question. Again they had three minutes to question and three minutes to respond to the question from a new individual across from them. Eventually, everyone had the opportunity to answer their own question. The process continued for six-minute rounds until all the participants had gathered information from six people and had had an opportunity to respond to all six questions, including their own. And in the process, each individual had become somewhat of an expert on his or her own question.

Figure 7-6: The Physical Layout of the Interview Design

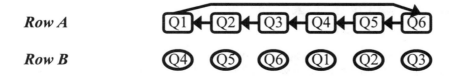

Following are the six questions chosen to generate the information necessary for the initial phase of the strategic planning process.

1. What three operational factors most inhibit our present productivity and our ability to reach our organizational goals?
2. How, if at all, should our current mission be altered to insure the best use of our organizational resources while still maintaining our corporate values?
3. What currently inhibits management from being as effective as possible (structure, staffing, methods)?
4. Considering our organization in ten years, what operational changes do you envision occurring in order for us to be increasingly successful?
5. What do we do that represents our greatest strength, which we should recognize and strive to maintain?
6. What values do we talk (act like we believe) but seldom walk in this organization?

After the interviews were completed, fifteen minutes was allotted for individuals to organize their data into what could be called:

*   *Truths* -- four, five or six people agreeing on an idea or response to a question.
*   *Trends* -- two or three people agreeing on an idea or response.
*   *Unique ideas* -- creative, original thoughts that warrant the attention of the participants.

At this point, all the people with Question 1 joined together in a group and were asked to discuss their data. The twelve people present selected a recorder to post the outcomes of their deliberations. They had one hour to complete two tasks. The first was to integrate their individual findings into a group consensus. Thus, they had to decide what information was worth bringing back to the total group as a truth or trend. In this case, at least eight of twelve would suffice to signify a truth. But a particular idea might be a truth for six people and a trend for six. If that occurred, the group had to reach consensus on the idea's significance. Similarly, the group had to agree on trends and any unique ideas they believed warranted the consideration of the total group.

Evaluation

There are a variety of theoretically sound reasons why this structured large group design works effectively with a variety of organizational goals.

1. The interviewing process is totally engaging. The participants are usually candid, because they realize that everyone else is answering the same questions and that their own responses have the potential to influence the outcome.
2. The fact that all have an opportunity to express their own views on each question is unique, and it yields a 100 percent sample during a forty minute activity. The process represents an extremely efficient use of both time and human resources.

3. There are usually a number of "facts" that arise from the integration and analysis of each question. A natural consensus evolves. People feel involved and empowered.

4. The process itself is difficult to manipulate even when one or two individuals bias their own note taking and interpretations of the data they gathered from their interviews. During the group discussion, the process itself is so public and consistent that individuals who might otherwise try to manipulate or influence the process are unwilling to compromise themselves in the face of such an open climate.

5. People feel "heard" even when their ideas don't make it to the status of fact, trend, or unique idea. The interview demands that each individual being interviewed receive 100 percent of someone's attention -- a rare experience for many.

6. The effective use of time and people is so far superior to what occurs in most meetings that evaluations are predictably very high and comments inevitably suggest the desire for additional meetings of this kind.

Chapter 8

Developing Solutions and Gaining Acceptance

Thus far, we have provided a framework for small business consulting, emphasizing the importance of personal relationships and team-building strategies, as well as careful project planning and management. We have emphasized how consulting to a small business differs from consulting with large corporations, made suggestions for obtaining data relevant to small business consulting, and examined the need for strategic thinking. Now we turn to the concepts and guidelines for developing solutions and gaining the acceptance of your small business client.

Developing Solutions: Creativity and Decision-making

Two capabilities are needed to develop good solutions to a problem. The first is the application of *creativity* to generate a sufficient number of effective alternatives. The second is the ability to use *good decision processes* in choosing among these alternatives. In other words, the ability to decide which alternative best fits the client's situation. Creativity works to *expand* the thinking of the client, while decision-making processes help to narrow and bring *focus* to the client's options. Both capabilities are necessary but not sufficient requirements for successful consulting. In addition, one must know when to be creative and when to make choices. Knowing when and how to apply these capabilities in a balanced manner is a challenge.

Creativity requires an expansiveness in thinking; a willingness to suspend evaluation and to entertain ideas that may not immediately make sense. It requires the ability to entertain an idea that at first glance may not appear to have any chance of working. On the other hand, good decision-making requires that one knows clearly the objectives, and that one evaluate accurately the consequences (both positive and negative) of each alternative. Accurate evaluation presupposes sound criteria for selecting one alternative over another, along with a tolerance for uncertainty and ambiguity. In management consulting, as in any complex business decision-making scenario, risk is inherent, and uncertainty and ambiguity are ever present.

Creativity and decision-making skills must be applied in a way that fits the client's problem. It is not helpful to the client if a consultant adds creativity to the situation when

---

the client has many, good alternatives. Such a situation calls for good decision-making. As consultants to small business, we must keep an eye on the strategic objectives and tactical necessities facing the small business client, and apply creativity and decision-making according to the client's need.

Creativity, Decision-Making And Critical Factors Facing Small Businesses

In chapter two, we identified critical "external constraints" for small businesses, including: access to data, or more accurately, the inability to obtain data, and increasing needs for training and development. We also cited key "internal factors", such as the insufficient strategic planning, the availability and use of technology, the client's inexperience with consultants, and resource or financial constraints. The diagram used in chapter two is reproduced below as Figure 8-1. These internal and external factors are often the cause of client problems. The ability to know when and how to apply creativity and when and how to add to the client's decision-making skill is discussed below with respect to the critical factors in Figure 8-1.

Figure 8-1: Critical Factors Facing Small Businesses

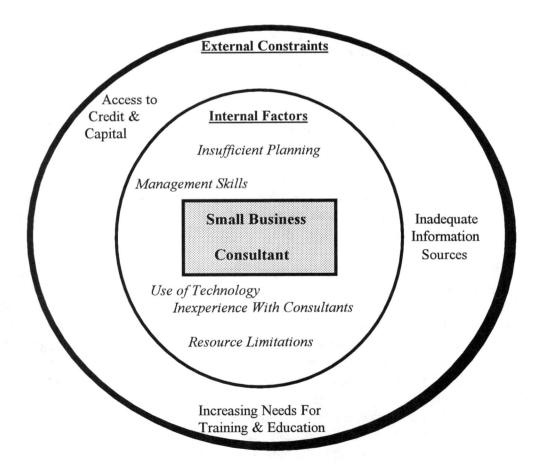

In order to increase your ability to recognize the critical factor, and as importantly, to know how to balance the application of creativity and decision-making skills, we will describe a situation and an appropriate consulting intervention or "solution" for that situation. While all situations will not be the same as those described here, these situations are sufficiently generic and common that you should be able to use the similarities between the situations described here and those that you encounter in your consulting work. The same is true for the solutions provided. The solutions will serve as useful analogies and help guide you in your decision with respect to the following questions:

- What *critical factor(s)* do my clients need to address in order to meet their objectives?
- Does my client need to apply more *creativity* in order to solve the problem with respect to this critical factor? (i.e., expand thinking).
- Does my client need to apply more *decision-making* skill in order to solve the problem with respect to this critical factor? (i.e., focus thinking).

Client's Critical Factor: Access To Data

Critical Factor	Expansion: Creativity/ Exploration	Focus: Effective Decision-Making
Access To Data	Lack of data has become a barrier to success: • reframing the problem • finding additional data sources • making new inferences from existing data.	Data exists but it is unclear how to use it: • extending mindsets through analogy and metaphor • structured decision-making

Situation: Lack of Data - Need for a New Point of View

In this situation the client and consultant are stuck! After an exhaustive search, and with the full expenditure of the resources available, there is no apparent solution with the data or information that is at hand. In summary, you find yourself "out of time, out of money, without a clue about what to do." Emotions provide important information in assessing what situation one faces. Here the emotion is typically frustration. One also tends to feel tired but knowledgeable about all the things that did not work. After a great deal of research, it is clear that you and your client are in the No Data; Need Creativity situation.

Possible Solution No. 1: Reframing Through Reversal. If at all possible, take time out. Almost all creative processes have a frustration stage. It is useful to take time out and allow all that you and your client have learned to "cook." Take time to relax. Do things that are *not* related to the problem. While you are off doing other things, your unconscious mental processes are working at rearranging what and how you think about the situation. Some of the most well known discoveries have come to people when resting from the work. At times the solution has even occurred during a dream.

Another useful technique is to reframe the problem, that is, dissolve the problem by challenging and changing assumptions (Bolman & Deal, 1997). Re-ask the questions that your have already answered. This time, work with the answer that you rejected as wrong. Assume that the answer that you rejected is correct. Play with the consequences of this reversal for awhile. See where it takes you.

This is essentially what Einstein did in discovering the Theory of Relativity. Despite Michelson and Morely's experiments to the contrary, at the turn of the 20th century, all scientists assumed that the speed of light could not be constant. For if the speed of light were constant, then time and space would have to be relative and not absolute. Einstein, for a moment, asked what if the experiment was true? What would be the consequences of working with that assumption? You know the rest of the story.

Continuing to work within the confines of the prevailing assumptions and "knowledge framework" or paradigm, frequently prevents the discovery of creative solutions (Kuhn, 1962). New perspectives may reveal new sources of data, a new problem definition, or a new use of the data that is available.

Situation: Lack of Data Due To Little or No Search Effort

The client and consultant have not "done their home work." There is no time to do the research that must be done to know what is going on. The "no time" position is taken despite the fact that little or no time has been allowed to determine if information is available. This is often described as "shooting from the hip." This situation is recognized by comments such as; "I don't have the time to look for all that stuff..." "In business we have to make decisions quickly..." "My intuition seldom fails me..." My gut tells me..." This may be true, and it is also true that clients in this situation can frequently benefit from additional facts.

Possible Solution No. 2: Systematic Search. Take the time to do the research. Look to the library, especially the business reference desk. Contact other businesses in the industry; contact trade unions and trade associations; use the Internet. Read chapter six of this book. Lend friends and any one else your ear. In summary, find additional data sources. If it is obvious that information is needed and that it has been prejudged that most is already known, then one service you can provide is to confirm intuition with facts. Your client may learn something new and valuable from your efforts.

Possible Solution No. 3: New Inferences From Existing Data. In Reframing (Solution No. 1), we attempt to re-think the problem, that is, to examine how we might see the problem through "new lenses" by reversing our assumptions and predisposition about the problem. In this solution we employ a conceptually similar technique, however, we apply it to the data rather than the problem. Leaving the problem as it is, how can we gain new insights and new ways to see the data?

One suggestion is to assume that you can have, and do have, any data that you want. Assume that all the information is available to you. Working within this assumption, describe in the most concrete and specific manner, the data that you want. Be sure that you specify the units (e.g., dollars/unit), the time period (monthly for the years ...), etc. Once you have committed this "data" to paper examine the information that you have. Can you approximate the data that you want? For example, can you combine an overall average (e.g., average sales/unit) and, by assuming it applies to all geography for which you have sales volume, develop an estimate of total sales dollars based on this average pricing? This simple example may not be classified as exceptionally creative, but frequently people will do without information that is "not available" rather than creatively derive estimates that would work much better than no data at all.

Situation: Data Is Available ... But How to Use It?

Disciplined research has been done. Time and money are truly at an end, and effort has not been the real reason for the lack of data availability. In this situation it seem as if data is plentiful but most, if not all of it, is irrelevant.

Possible Solution No. 1: Extending Mindset Through Analogy and Metaphor. This solution is similar to reframing, but it is not as direct or as general a suggestion as reframing. Here the task is to make new inferences from existing data. Can the information available be used by analogy; that is, does it reveal information about another company or industry that has similarities to the client's company or industry and therefore can be extended to your client's situation? The information becomes useful and relevant by extension, that is, by analogy (Morgan, 1997).

A type of extension of data is the metaphor. A metaphor is a story or a situation, often hypothetical, that must be creatively constructed to see the similarities and useful extension from the metaphor to the situation at hand. A metaphor can be thought of as a fictional analogy. It is a way to facilitate the reframing needed for additional creativity.

An example may be helpful. One company wanted to decentralize the production scheduling function. In order to do so, new ways of reporting information had to be created, to allow the locus of decision-making to shift from the main office to the four regional offices. No one involved in the current system could imagine how to make the information available to regional personnel without duplicating the same information at the central scheduling location. The boundary between the two groups of people was confusing - too much redundant data, too many overlapping decisions, in too many locations.

To simplify the conceptualization of this problem, a "check book" metaphor was used. The regional personnel simply kept a detailed check book balance. At the end of each month, each region gave the central scheduling function the final balance by product. This allowed the central scheduling group to make changes in company-wide capacity or to broker the excesses and shortages between regions without doing the detailed scheduling.

Possible Solution No. 2: Structured Decision-making. When data exists but it is unclear how to use it, the added clarity of a structured decision-making process is most helpful. Table 8-1 is an outline of a seven step decision-making process that may be useful in this situation. The objective of the process is clarity with respect to each aspect of a decision, and the context for that decision.

Table 8-1: A Structured Decision-Making Process

- *Analyze the Situation:* Identify and describe the client's situation as fully as possible. This provides information for establishing objectives.

- *Establish Objectives/ Describe End State::* What does the client want to achieve, the ultimate outcome that the client wants to create. This should also be as concrete as possible.

- *Generate Alternatives:* The outcome of this step is to have a rich set of alternative ways to obtain the client's objective(s) and to create the end state that is envisioned. It is important not to short cut this step due to impatience, frustration, premature evaluation, or other reasons that do not contribute to achieving the goal.

- *Establish Criteria:* At this stage of the decision-making process, one must establish the criteria against which each alternative will be evaluated. The criteria should be comprehensive. It is suggested that the criteria include financial, personal, social, strategic, time, and risk dimensions. The concept of the "balanced scorecard" from chapter seven may be a useful framework for establishing criteria.

- *Evaluate Alternatives:* In the evaluation stage, one must determine how each alternative fits the criteria established. It is usually helpful to rank the alternatives if a number of alternatives are being evaluated and, depending on the nature of the problem, to assign some numerical weight.

- *Make A Decision:* Choose the alternative that best fits the criteria. In addition, does the alternative pass the "gut test," that is, is it intuitively sound, or does the consultant or client feel that there may be something wrong with this alternative. If an alternative is highly preferred analytically but does not pass the gut test then a discussion to discover the cause of the discomfort with respect to the decision outcome is appropriate. Do not go forward on important, high stakes decisions unless the choice is positive on both an analytical and intuitive basis.

- *Establish Feedback Mechanism:* Even the best decision processes do not guarantee a positive outcome. Therefore, it is important to establish a feedback or learning mechanism as part of any decision. Identify the type of information needed to determine the accuracy of the decision.

Client's Critical Factor: Lack of Strategic Thinking/ Short-Term Orientation

Critical Factor	Expansion: Creativity/ Exploration	Focus: Effective Decision-Making
Time Orientation Short V. Long	The pressure of short-term deadlines prevail and this stems from an attitude of "we don't have time to do it right; only to do it over..." The root cause is the lack of alternatives.	The pressure of short-term deadlines prevails and this stems from the mindset that there are an overwhelming number of options or activities to consider.

Situation: Short-Term Pressures Override Strategic Thinking

In this client situation, the pressure of short-term considerations, deadlines, or resource pressures overwhelm any effective management or strategic planning. The root cause of this behavior is best expressed by the attitude, "We don't have time to do it that way..." It is more accurately expressed by the cliché, "We don't have time to do it right; only to do it over again." Here the root cause of ineffectiveness or inefficiency is the lack of alternatives and the absence of creativity. This situation is most prevalent when scarcity of resources, such as time and money, comes to dominate the thinking of the small business owner or team. This scarcity is almost always present in small businesses, but it does not always dominate the thinking and cause the lack of creativity that we are describing here. A combination of Type A personality and a shortage of critical resources are often the chemistry that creates this potential explosion.

Possible Solution No. 1: Seek a Series of Small Wins. An effective way to make progress with a client who is short-term oriented is to create an early win. Changing a client's mindset from short-term to longer-term is difficult since the change runs contrary to a life-long experience which the client believes has been effective. That is, clients often believe that this short-term orientation is necessary and has contributed to their success; the mindset is deeply entrenched. Change can be achieved by a demonstration of success with a new, more balanced approach. This must be demonstrated, not merely discussed. The consultant must be sure to create small wins through frequent "pay days" for the client. That is, the project must be set up in small milestones, and it must be made clear that the milestone has been reached and the benefits obtained. It is also important to try to communicate that the milestone is a part of a larger context. The consultant may or may not be successful at establishing this larger context in the mind of the client. If it can be done, then it may impart a valuable capability to the client organization. If it cannot be done, then at least a series of somewhat isolated successes have been achieved.

Possible Solution No. 2: Add Structure and Make The Alternatives Manageable. The critical task in this solution is to apply a structure to the seemingly overwhelming number of options available to the client. One structure could be grouping or "chunking" the alternatives into related categories and evaluating the categories as a whole. This will at least reduce the number of alternatives that need to be evaluated in detail.

A second possibility is to create procedural or process structure. The decision-making process outlined in Table 8-1 is one way to add structure to the process of coping with many -- seemingly too many -- alternatives. One must be careful not to be too rigorous, or the process will bog down and turn into "analysis paralysis." With proper attention to the reaction of the client to one's process recommendation, it is almost certain that process structure will be beneficial to the client organization.

Client's Critical Factor: Management Skills

Critical Factor	Expansion: Creativity/ Exploration	Focus: Effective Decision-Making
Management Skills	Lack management skills and knowledge: seek training, coaching, development, hiring, temporary help.	Management skills are present but poorly applied, the structured managing process has failed: provide feedback.

Situation: Lack Management Skills and Knowledge

In this situation, there is a clear lack of skill or knowledge within the client organization. This is most easily seen as a sin of omission, that is, the client organization just does not do or pay attention to the area requiring the specific skill. If financial knowledge is deficient, then you will know this by what is missing in the organization. There will be no budget, no cash management, poor control and accounting for resources. If marketing is the deficient skill, there will be no apparent marketing strategy or sales plan, for example. When looking for the absent knowledge and skill areas, determine what is not being done in the organization.

Solution: Training, Coaching, Development, Hiring, Temporary Help. Training, coaching and development will bolster management skills and knowledge, and provide insights for creativity. The most obvious corrective step is to initiate training. Coaching by a knowledgeable or skilled coworker or supervisor, or a longer-term personnel development strategy for the organization are often needed. The difficulty with this suggestion lies in the time and resources required. The payoffs are real but often difficult to measure. If this solution is judged to be the recommendation, then be sure to establish learning objectives that are concrete and measurable. Connect the learning objective to meaningful improvements in business operations. Finally, in every instance in which it is possible, measure the improvements in operations and provide feedback on the outcomes, both positive and negative.

Situation: Management Skill Poorly Applied

If the management skills are present but poorly applied, then some stage of the management process has failed. This situation is evident when the client provides a history of why a particular recommendation cannot work in this unique situation. As a consultant you cannot dismiss this information. Nonetheless, frequent "been there, done that" reactions to suggestions may be symptomatic of an underlying resistance to change. This resistance may originate from an anxiety about change or a lack of confidence in the face of a new endeavor.

Solution: Provide Feedback. Feedback is required when the source of the problem is the failure to apply existing management skills and knowledge. Feedback can be a stimulus for change. The best feedback is information generated by the person or department that must make the change. People do not argue with their own data. Conversely, if the desire to resist change is sufficiently strong, it is easier to argue with the consultant's data than it is to make the needed changes, as we have stated in chapter five. To be most successful, feedback should be immediate, specific, and if possible, provide insight into the origin of the problem and potential corrective actions.

Client's Critical Factor: Use Of, or Access To, Technology

Critical Factor	Expansion: Creativity/ Exploration	Focus: Effective Decision-Making
Access to Technology	No technological options ... a feeling of powerlessness.	Confusion: a willingness and ability to use but inability to choose.

Situation: No Technological Options

A client in this situation believes that no technological options are available to the organization, which is rapidly being passed by as the technology advances. It may be difficult to assess the cause of the feeling of helplessness or powerlessness often expressed by the client. Fortunately, one can often proceed with a successful recommendation without knowing the psychology of the client's views about technology. In some situations, the client is unable to obtain a technology that is critical to the organization's success. This may be due to resource limitations (cash), patents, or lack of knowledge.

Solution: Niche Strategy. If technological options are truly not available to the small business client, then the client must provide a product or service to his customer that cannot be provided by firms with access to technology. This entails a change in strategy and the need to focus on a niche. For example, a medium to large sized firm may be able to afford a sophisticated materials handling system that provides for the efficient handling and shipment of fully loaded trucks. The extended lead-time required with this type of system might well create a service niche for a small firm that has more flexibility. The small firm may provide mixed cases or emergency ordering service or other customized services that cannot be offered by the more highly automated firm. Essentially, this is a war avoidance strategy. One must be fairly certain that the competitive niche will endure long enough to pay back any investment made by the client organization.

Situation: Confusion About Technology

We were recently contacted by a small business specializing in vending programs and concessions at amusement parks across the country. They needed to find "a computer data base program that would link all of the parks and process sales information". Under the current system, on-site managers completed the sales paperwork by hand and faxed it to the head office. In turn, the data was manually entered into the computers at the head office. Here the client has the resources to gain access to the technology but is simply not sufficiently informed to be able to make the right choice. This is a common situation, most likely to arise in technological areas that are ancillary to the main endeavor of the small business. For example, a small business may have a core competency in the flexible manufacture of a product, but may not have the competency in order processing systems. It is possible that a good technological position is important in a support function that might not be considered the most critical function in the small business.

Solution: Acquire Knowledge And Structure Decision-Making Process. This solution is similar to those suggested previously. The difference in this situation is that knowledge required often does not need to be maintained in the small business organization on a continuing basis. The knowledge is best purchased from a provider that has this technology as their main expertise. The most common examples of this practice are found in the professions, that is, engineering, accounting, law, and information technology.

Client's Critical Factor: Inexperience With or Resistance to Consulting

Critical Factor	Expansion: Creativity/ Exploration	Focus: Effective Decision-Making
Mindset on Consulting	Consultants viewed as a waste of time. Exploration of successes.	Inability to match consultant and problem. Project Proposal - Deliverables.

Situation: Consultants Viewed As A Waste Of Time

Some small business managers view consultants as a luxury, or worse yet, as a waste of time. Fortunately, this situation is not frequently encountered, not because it is rare but because those who hold these views are unlikely to even discuss consulting possibilities.

Solution: Exploration of Successful Consulting Intervention Is Needed. If you are determined to initiate a consulting intervention with a client in this situation, then you are well advised to be prepared to demonstrate how valuable the consulting engagement will be to the client. Have a series of successful interventions to draw from -- provide a list of references; be prepared to relate these experiences to the potential client's business. These testimonials are appropriate for any client. Indeed, if the consultant's list of potential clients is large enough, he/she should apply the effort to more promising clients. The solution suggested here would be more effective with a client who is less rigid and less negative about the help that can be provided by a consulting intervention.

Situation: Inability To Match Consultant and Problem

Here the client is unable to describe the problem and/or identify the right consulting organization.

Solution: Project Proposal - Deliverables. The steps suggested for the "unbelieving" client will work well with this client. In addition, providing a project proposal (see chapter five) will be helpful. The deliverables section of the proposal should be especially helpful since it describes the concrete outcomes of the project as it affects the client's business. This should make the other aspects of a well-written proposal very relevant to the client, and clearly establish the overall benefits of the engagement.

Client's Critical Factor: Limited Resources & Finances

Critical Factor	Expansion: Creativity/ Exploration	Focus: Effective Decision-Making
Resources & Finances	Victim of resource limitations.	Inability to apply resources effectively or efficiently.

Situation: Victim of Resource Limitations

This is a most common situation for small businesses. As discussed in chapter two, one of the major causes of small business failure is insufficient capitalization. Another major cause of the failure of small businesses is the lack of management skill, which can also be viewed as a limit on resources.

Solution: Deferred Spending, Loans. If you find a start-up business with severe resources limitations, it is a most difficult situation to salvage. Occasionally, one can defer spending plans to conserve cash. Pricing increases are a possibility, if the competitive market allows. Securing additional cash through conventional financing is best done when one does not need the money. Ironically, conventional lenders do not lend money to small businesses that really need it because of their traditionally low tolerance for risk. If the resource limitations are skills and knowledge, then the temporary addition of technical or management expertise, possibly through the SBA, is a possibility.

Situation: Inability to Apply Resources Effectively or Efficiently

Here resources are available but they are wasted, either because they are not being applied to the right work or they are being squandered. The outcomes generated by the expenditure are needed, but they are not being generated at a high enough output to input ratio. The costs are too high when compared to the benefits obtained.

Solution: Accounting and Control Systems. In this situation, management systems need special attention, particularly the client's planning and control systems.

Table 8-2 provides a summary of the critical factors facing small businesses and lists those situations that point to more creativity and those which usually call for more structured and effective decision-making processes. While the situations encountered will not be exactly like those described here, the similarities may provide general guidelines and food for thought for applying the suggested solutions.

Table 8-2: Summary

Critical Factor	Expansion: Creativity / Exploration	Focus: Effective Decision-Making
Access To Data	Problem: Lack of data has become a barrier to success. Solution: reframe the problem, find additional data sources, or make new inferences from existing data.	Problem: Data exists but it is unclear how to use it. Solution: Extending mindsets through analogy and metaphor, and structured decision-making.
Time Orientation Short V. Long	Problem: Pressure of short-term deadlines or resource pressures leads to poor decisions ... "we don't have time to do it right; only to do it over ..." Solution: If the root cause is the lack of alternatives, add creativity. Prove the value of creativity.	Problem: The pressure of short-term deadlines or resource pressures leads to poor decisions. Solution: If the root cause is an overwhelming number of options or activities, then a focused decision-making process is needed.
Management Skills	Problem: Skills and knowledge missing. Solution: Training and coaching will develop management skills and knowledge.	Problem: Management skills are present but poorly applied ... some stage of the decision-making process has failed. Solution: Specific feedback is an excellent source of motivation for improved decision-making.
Access To Technology	Problem: No technological options ... a feeling of powerlessness. Solution: Search for technological alternatives; benchmarking, competitive analysis, industry research ...	Problem: Confusion, a willingness and ability to use, but inability to choose technology. Solution: Clear articulation of business needs along with pros and cons of alternatives.

Mindset On Consulting	Problem: Consultants viewed as a waste of time. Solution: Demonstrate successful consulting interventions.	Problem: Inability to match consultant and problem. Solution: Well-written project proposal - with objectives, methods, and deliverables.
Resources & Finances	Problem: Victim of resource limitations including cash. Solution: Search for greater efficiency within organization, and simultaneous search for outside resources.	Problem: Inability to apply resources effectively or efficiently. Solution: Clearly articulate strategy and plan with objectives, methods, expected quantitative and qualitative outcomes.

The Creative Process

Small businesses frequently find their competitive advantage in their ability to respond quickly and creatively to customer needs. But how can the consultant introduce more creativity into a small business consultation? The question of organizational learning was addressed in chapter seven. Here we add to that discussion with a focus on creativity.

The first step in creativity is breaking out of existing mindsets, playing with ideas and allowing them to ruminate. Negative evaluations will stifle the free-flow of ideas before they have been explored to some degree. Rules for fostering creativity include:

- Encourage idea generation.
- Keep ideas on the surface and visible.
- Do not allow immediate evaluation of ideas (suspend judgment).

The second step in the creative process is to play with the new ideas for a sufficiently long time, allowing possibilities or alternatives to develop. Thoughts or actions that short-circuit creativity include premature closure on alternative generation, and emotions that create doubt and negativity. One CEO decided to forbid any of his executive staff from bringing calculators into strategy meetings because of their penchant to reject ideas before they were sufficiently developed, based on simple financial analyses.

Finally, since creativity entails risk, an assessment must be made of how much creativity is appropriate for the client and the client's situation. Consultants should outline the choices as objectively and as clearly as possible, and let the client decide how much creativity or risk to take.

Making Good Recommendations

In order to make good recommendations, a number of things are necessary, including:

- Clear objectives and goals.
- A rich set of alternatives.
- Relevant criteria.
- Effective evaluation of alternatives.
- Clear decision.
- Clear statement of the consequences.

A Rich Set of Clear Alternatives

It is said that most of creativity is in the questions asked. Questions that result in a rich set of alternatives are most useful in advancing the creativity needed to produce sound recommendations. Without consideration of a range of alternatives, recommendations will tend to be narrow and lack robustness; that is, they will be subject to change with the slightest change in environment or circumstance. Those without time for considering a range of alternative recommendations are frequently sentenced to solving the same problem over again.

Clear Objectives and Relevant Criteria

Clear objectives and goals are needed as a basis for judging the efficacy of the alternatives and the relevance of the criteria. Objectives are action-directed outcomes, which are measurable and time-bounded. A format for creating action-oriented objectives is shown in Table 8-3.

Table 8-3: Creating Action-Oriented Objectives

Action	What	When
to create	new product or program	within 10 months
to develop	new customer segments	by August 1st
to achieve	quality standards	by Wednesday
to master	a process	tomorrow

It is useful to distinguish between two types of criteria: *End-State Criteria,* that is, criteria that define the attainment of one's objectives and goals, and *Means Criteria,* that is, criteria that specifies the conditions that are necessary and sufficient to achieving the objectives and goals. The End-State Criteria indicate when the ultimate objective or goal has been achieved, while the Means Criteria may be used as standards to measure the extent to which the approach to the objectives has been efficacious. Accurately specifying the means that are necessary and sufficient to achieve a desired end is obviously critical to success. However, the determination of this in business and most other endeavors is often more an art than a science. Clearly distinguishing between End-State and Means Criteria may help.

Consider a familiar example involving financial planning. If a client aspires to financial wealth, there are a number of necessary and sufficient conditions that define financial wealth and another set that one believes will result in the attainment of financial wealth for the client. The End-State and Means Criteria in this example might be as follows:

End-State Criteria
- To achieve Net Income of $100,000 per year
- To establish Net Worth of $1,000,000
- To maintain maximum indebtedness below $250,000
- To minimize risk to income by having at least three customer accounts of $20,000 each

Means Criteria
1. To build family business by 50% over two years.
2. To advertise twice per year in TV Guide Magazine.
3. To hire a sales person to call on catalogue dealers.
4. To provide training in new customer service software package.
5. To save 10% of after-tax earnings.

Criteria are established at the level of detail that is judged to be appropriate, so that the success of the means being employed may be monitored as quickly and as reliably as possible.

Effective Evaluation of Alternatives

In order to evaluate alternatives, one must estimate the impact of the alternative on the Means and/or End-State Criteria. One must also have a subjective assessment or explicit probability estimate for the likelihood that the payoff from the alternative is as predicted. The reliable payoff and risk assessments are imperative. If these are not available, the risk dimension of the alternative becomes uncertain, and must be judged accordingly. This is demonstrated below in Table 8-4.

Clear Decision

Once a decision is made, it is important to communicate very specifically the scope of that decision. The time taken to clarify the scope of a decision will avoid problems in the future. A common problem is a consultant's failure to clarify the time frame for the implementation of a decision. The client felt that implementation within 12 months would be acceptable. The consultant thought that two months was more than enough time to implement the change.

Clear Statement of the Consequences

The benefits and costs of a decision should be clearly specified as well. Enthusiasm may lead one to overemphasize the benefits or ignore the costs. However, it is critical to reveal the costs or additional risks that are a consequence of a decision. Objectivity on this point may seem to dampen enthusiasm but it creates preparedness and builds trust.

Table 8-4 is designed to help make explicit the consequences of alternatives. Each recommendation should be thought through as to its effect on critical factors that most commonly effect small business clients. "Weight" represents the relative importance of one factor to another. We have used the critical factors here but any area that is judged to be important can be included. We could then assign a contribution of the alternative to each factor. In the example, we are using a scale of 0 to 10 for both weights on factors and impact of alternatives. A score of 10 reflects the greatest positive impact; zero indicates no impact. Negative numbers in the scale could also be included to indicate expected negative impacts.

In Table 8-4, the ranking of the alternative is obtained by multiplying the weight times the contribution of each alternative to that factor. Alternative #1 has a 300 rating, #2 has a 275 rating; #3 has a 200 rating, and #4 a 270 rating. These ratings are not meant to be used as the sole basis for making final decisions nor to supplant reasoned judgment. Rather, they are a way to gain additional information in the overall decision-making process.

Table 8-4: Evaluation of Alternatives Matrix

critical factors	Weight	Alternative #1	Alternative #2	Alternative #3	Alternative #4
access to data	5	10 $5 \times 10 = 50$	10 $5 \times 5 = 25$	10 $5 \times 10 = 50$	10 $5 \times 10 = 50$
time orientation short v. long	10	10 $10 \times 10 = 100$	10 $10 \times 5 = 50$	10 $10 \times 0 = 0$	2 $10 \times 2 = 20$
management skills	10	10 $10 \times 10 = 100$	10 $10 \times 10 = 100$	10 $10 \times 10 = 100$	10 $10 \times 10 = 100$
technology	5	0 $5 \times 0 = 0$	5 $5 \times 5 = 50$	0 $5 \times 0 = 0$	0 $5 \times 0 = 0$
mindset on consulting	0	0 $0 \times 0 = 0$	0 $0 \times 0 = 0$	0 $0 \times 0 = 0$	0 $0 \times 0 = 0$
resources & finances	10	5 $10 \times 5 = 50$	5 $10 \times 5 = 50$	5 $10 \times 5 = 50$	10 $10 \times 10 = 100$
other areas	0	0	0	0	0
TOTALS	40	300	275	200	270

Beliefs and Values

Finally, it is important to assess alternatives in view of their impact on your own beliefs and principles, and those of the client. Beliefs and values go beyond mere compliance with legal and regulatory issues, to questions of ethics and moral principles (see chapter three for the discussion of the ethics of consulting). Are alternative choices consistent with these beliefs and principles?

Conclusion

In this chapter we have examined the need for creativity and sound decision-making processes in developing recommendations for the small business client. We have used the critical factors of small business consulting identified in chapter two to anchor this discussion.

Implicit throughout this discussion is the need to develop recommendations that the client will embrace and implement. To increase one's chances of client acceptance, consider three issues. First, the processes described in this chapter and throughout the book are inclusive and collaborative; that is, they encourage the client's participation. Given that people are less inclined to argue with information that they generate and processes they contribute to, this inclusive approach will help foster client acceptance of recommendations.

Second, along with the participation of the client, the respect that the consultant grants to the client is obvious when using the approaches and recommendations in this book. This respect helps to build client/consultant trust and also fosters acceptance of recommendations. The importance of maintaining a client/consultant relationship based on mutual respect and trust should always remain paramount.

Finally, acceptance is facilitated when consultants understand different learning or information gathering styles and adapt their reports, presentations and general communication formats accordingly. The three principle modes of learning are visual, auditory, and experiential. If unaware of the preferred learning mode of the client, it is useful to present ideas in all three modes. For example, use a visual or picture, combined with the spoken word, and have the client participate in a sample problem or simulation that illustrates the point being made in the visual and auditory modes. It may require more work and more creativity to communicate in all three modalities, but it is an effective way to increase the likelihood that the client will receive the message that is intended.

References.

Bolman, Lee G. & Terrence E. Deal. 1997. *Reframing Organizations: Artistry, Choice and Leadership, 2nd edition*. San Francisco: Jossey-Bass.

Kuhn, Thomas S. 1962. *The Structure of Scientific Revolution, 2nd edition*. Chicago, IL: The University of Chicago Press.

Morgan, Garreth. 1997. *Images of Organization*. Thousand Oaks, CA: Sage Publications.

Appendix 1

Software for Project Management

Software packages are available to help the project management process run more smoothly. The purpose of Appendix 1 is to identify, compare and contrast several mid-level project management software applications, focusing on those that are most likely to meet the needs of the small business consultant.

Recall from chapter five that the small business consulting process typically moves through a series of predictable stages of development. We have introduced the EPIC Framework to describe these stages - Exploration, Preparation, Implementation and Conclusion. Project management software enables the small business consultant to more systematically plan and manage these stages. Furthermore, since projects seldom proceed precisely as planned, project management software also allows the user to monitor progress, adjust schedules, generate reports, and develop what-if scenarios.

Criteria For Selection Of Software

A checklist to assist companies in their selection of project management software was developed and published by *Fortune* (1997). Criteria used to make the decision are:

- *Scope* - Make sure that the software you choose matches your needs. If you plan to manage several projects at once, be sure the program supports multiproject operations and can share files such as calendars and data.

- *Organizational Requirements* - If you need to support many users, the software should enable them to share files, while providing security measures to safeguard data. The software should also work with the databases and software in use at your organization.

- *Implementation* - Project Management software can be complex. Be sure that after-sales services are available.

Comparison of Mid-Level Project Management Software Applications[*]

As one of the galaxies' best project managers, Darth Vader, said so eloquently to a nervous middle manager, "I've come to put you back on schedule." That is the essence of project management – to plan, observe, and evaluate projects so they are accomplished within the desired performance, dollars, and time parameters (the PDT objectives discussed in chapter five).

That is rarely an easy task; available resources in the small business, as we have said, often seem insufficient for the goals assigned. But project management software can help, with an array of well-integrated products designed for all levels of project complexity and project management experience.

Project management tools range from the miniature to-do modules found in contact managers or PIMs to super-powered applications like Primavera Systems' Primavera Project Planner for Windows. Four mid-range project managers that supply the tools necessary to create, track, and analyze the progress of any undertaking are reviewed below. Each furnishes sophisticated, automatic resource leveling; PERT charts and resource histograms to study workflow and task allocation; and macros, work codes, quick report generation, and quality graphics. Using one of these programs may facilitate project management.

CA-SuperProject 3.1

Computer Associates' program (CA-SuperProject's 3.1 release) provides, among other things, an on-line Help Assist Mode for continuous, real-time field help, resource and date outlining, effort-driven scheduling, time-scaled PERT charts, resource pooling, and linked project-cost charting. It also lets you click and drag to link tasks – a feature Symantec's Time Line 6.0 lacks.

At the core of CA-SuperProject 3.1 is Project Manager's Assistant, a help system similar to Microsoft applications' Wizards. Project Manager's Assistant demonstrates more than 80 procedures, showing instructions, advice, and tools for each in a clear outline format. A Fast Start section guides new users through the basic steps of project creation, from setting up a project calendar to outlining tasks and resources, estimating task durations, linking tasks, and so on. Less rigid than Microsoft Project's Wizards,

---

[*] This comparison of software packages is based on a class project developed by Jim Foley, Jim Keane, Shiv Hatti, Kathy Wilson, and especially Will May. The authors wish to thank them for their important contributions.

The purpose of this information is not to endorse any particular software package, but to provide information so that small business consultants may make their own informed choices.

Project Manager's Assistant allows you to add your own notes or include specific guidelines to help other users on a shared system or network.

The strength of CA-SuperProject's real-world modeling capabilities is formidable. Resource assignments can reflect different efficiency ratings. Resources produced within one task can be consumed within others. You can use 13 separate calculations to measure cost and schedule performance, including Earned Value, Cost Performance Index, and Calculated Estimate at Completion.

When it comes to task tracking and cost management, CA-SuperProject surpasses Microsoft Project 4.0. The program offers fewer charting options than the other project managers discussed here, but its date-specified resource leveling is excellent – faster than any of its rivals', if less detailed than the manual prioritizing offered by Scitor's Project Scheduler 6.

Multiple-project handling is a strong feature. CA-SuperProject provides resource pooling and lets you link one task to several projects. Tasks in one project can become predecessors to those in other projects, though none of this shows up on the Gantt chart.

Graphical mouse support creates task-precedence links (including Finish-Starts, Start-Starts, and Finish-Finish types) in version 3.1. Another ease-of-use enhancement, multilevel undo, will outdo anything in Microsoft Project or Time Line, though it will not be as extensive as that of Project Scheduler 6. An elegant solution to the screen clutter that bedevils Time Line's multiwindowed approach is provided – a Combined Projects View that presents all open projects on a single task outline, PERT chart, or WBS chart. Clicking tabs below the toolbar will let you select a project to edit.

Finally, new project-modeling tools will include ladder networks – two tasks with a start-to-start or finish-to-finish dependency – and the option to alter overtime into conflict hours. You can keep three sets of baselines in CA-SuperProject 3.1 rather than one – ideal for interim comparisons. A report-creating Form Report Assistant complements SuperProject's dozens of ready-made sample reports.

CA-SuperProject 3.1 is neither as feature-rich as Project Scheduler 6 nor as attentive to novice needs as Microsoft Project, but its combination of advanced features and tutorial assistance make for a product that can train new users quickly, yet keep them satisfied as they become veteran project managers. Based on past history, users can be assured of a strong upgrade path.

Microsoft Project 4.0

Many small business consultants will readily admit that their job performance could improve with the help of some project management tools, but not long ago, project management software was viewed as too complex and its terminology too obscure to appeal to the average user. When it entered the market, Microsoft decided to change that.

The result is Microsoft Project 4.0, with many features aimed squarely at novice users. It is not the most sophisticated project manager available, but it couples plenty of attractive features with the lowest learning curve in its class.

The differences are apparent as soon as the program loads. You are welcomed by the Planning Wizard, one of Microsoft's help tools that differ from the standard Windows help system in their multiple-branching, pick-and-choose options. For example, the Planning Wizard will provide specific assistance in building a task/duration list or resource assignment, instead of forcing you to sit through an entire tutorial about basic project design. Of course, you can always choose a complete tutorial; there are many extensive ones available in Project 4.0.

The Wizard help system has an additional dimension as well; you can request more in-depth instruction at any point, getting anything from a few extra hints to a full-screen, captioned procedural diagram with object links to pop-up definitions. On the minus side, the Wizard system loads as a separate program from Microsoft Project, and by default floats to the front of the screen. This makes it easy to follow along, but it can interfere with multitasking.

In other friendly features, ToolTips show a one-word description of a button's purpose whenever you point to it. Context-sensitive shortcut menus are available with a click of the right mouse button, and complex dialog boxes are neatly subdivided into tabbed subject screens. Other changes in Microsoft Project 4.0 will impress hard-bitten project managers as well as novices. The program can merge up to 80 projects and all their details. Similarly, resource pools can be shared by up to 80 project files.

A new Resource Management View combines a spreadsheet-like resource workload summary (a list of people viewed against their committed time) with a Gantt chart that emphasizes task assignment. Highlight a person to see over-assigned hours, and the Gantt chart automatically displays his or her task commitments. This makes it much easier to pinpoint workload difficulties than traditional resource histogram displays.

Microsoft Project's many preconfigured views have the advantage of being gathered under a single menu category; programs such as Project Scheduler 6 and CA-SuperProject group them according to function. After you have found the Project tables you want, however, you may not know how to proceed: Microsoft falls back here and in other advanced areas on its older help system rather than Wizards. It takes a search through several help submenus to find a descriptive list of available tables.

Project is not officially part of the Microsoft Office suite, but has family ties to other Redmond applications: A Send Task Requests feature permits workgroup participants to accept or decline tasks via Microsoft Mail, and after a worker commits to a task, it is automatically added to his or her Microsoft Schedule+ task file.

Microsoft's tech support is excellent, but Project's written documentation is not up to par. All the reference materials are on-line, not printed; the enclosed User's Guide will get you up and running, but you may only get to the corner of the first block. Project also continues to lag behind other project managers in several technically oriented ways. It cannot perform overtime calculations on a task-by-task basis, for instance, or apply customized calendars to both tasks and resources. Nor is there a PERT analysis to create multiple what-if scenarios of duration and cost.

Still, with release 4.0, Microsoft Project takes a well-defined and prominent position in the field. Its exceptionally intuitive interface, novice hand-holding, and overall ease of use make it a top choice for a workgroup with little or no project management experience, while it offers more than enough sophisticated tools to keep any project team from outgrowing the program before its next upgrade.

Scitor Project Scheduler 6 Version 1.5

Conventional wisdom dictates that you get what you pay for. Scitor's Project Scheduler 6 may be an exception to the rule, with a mid-range price but many high-end features.

Like the other project managers reviewed here, Project Scheduler 6 lets you optionally define Work Breakdown Structure (WBS) and Organizational Breakdown Structure (OBS) codes for all tasks as two ways of distinguishing their hierarchical relationships. Project Scheduler 6 additionally supports RBS (Resource Breakdown Structure) codes, which supply a handy classification method and filtering tool for resource assignment and reporting.

Another example of Project Scheduler's high-end functionality is its second-generation Open Database Connectivity (ODBC) support, which lets you export or import specific project data fields to other ODBC-capable networking applications such as spreadsheets and relational databases. The other three project managers here offer only first-generation ODBC support, which means you must transfer entire projects. That is fine for relatively small projects, but as projects grow and merge, such transfers rapidly become unwieldy, and their reconfiguration in the new application becomes a nightmare.

You can record these export commands to create an iconized batch file in Project Scheduler's program group. It is an easy way to send updated project materials to your workgroup members. The same automation procedure also works for more complex operations.

Despite its many options, the program is not difficult to operate or comprehend. You can enter Budgeted Cost of Work Performed/Scheduled, check the Can Split box to separate and move forward the remaining portion of a partially completed task, or prioritize tasks on a scale of 0 to 9,999 for ultra-detailed control of resource leveling. Or you can work in reverse, and use the advanced spreadsheet as a complete tracking mechanism. It is an easy way to print, display, and export project data to your coworkers without having to explain what Gantt bars and PERT nodes mean. Everything is listed under an appropriate category heading, from a given task's percentage of cost variance to its total float.

Simple cut, copy, and paste commands make working with spreadsheet cells in Project Scheduler very easy. The program also supplies unlimited undo and redo--a lifesaver when you realize that a fully configured task you eliminated from the project 10 minutes ago was necessary, after all.

Most impressive of all, however, is Project Scheduler's ability to meet advanced project management needs. No other program in this price range offers so many options that conform to real-world conditions. Take cost management, for example: What if the wholesale prices of all your resources purchased from Acme Distributors changed in mid-project due to inflation? Most project managers would require you to re-enter the resource costs manually, but Project Scheduler lets you simply apply an inflation schedule. In fact, you can save up to 10 inflation schedules and five alternate costs per resource.

Project Scheduler's PERT probability-analysis chart is equally impressive. It is a graphical reporting tool that displays the likelihood of projects finishing on time and within cost under different sets of circumstances. You define three groups of duration estimates for all tasks, and Project Scheduler quickly builds a tricolor diagram of the best, worst, and most likely scenarios. If project management may seem at times like endlessly working toward an unreachable goal, this tool may provide the reassurance your workgroup needs.

Scitor's written documentation and tech support are excellent. On-line help is good, and the version 1.5 upgrade supplies Microsoft-like tool tips. Overall, Project Scheduler 6 should lay a strong claim on your interest if you want the most project management power for your dollar.

Time Line 6.0

Time Line users who were bitterly disappointed by the product's uninspiring Windows debut have reason to be pleased with the version 6.0. Time Line has been completely redesigned, with many features that place it squarely in the front rank of medium-priced project managers.

The changes are visible at every level. Multiple project links, for example, allow you to attach a single task to multiple projects or project summaries in the same database. Resources can maintain individual availability profiles, split tasks around vacations and other non-project-related events, and perform individual tasks allocated to several different projects.

The first Time Line for Windows was incapable of effectively managing even elementary task conflicts concerning over-allocated resources, but resource leveling has improved dramatically in Time Line 6.0. OLE client/server support has also been added, as well as first-generation ODBC support. Network security remains rudimentary, however, consisting only of read-only and write-only passwords for a database. Time Line's three competitors are not much better, but at least they let you assign passwords on a project-by-project basis. Reports, too, continue to present a problem in Time Line 6.0. You get 33 report types, but cannot customize them, apply formulas, or create new reports as you can with the competition – unless, that is, you purchase Time Line Report Maker.

The changes in Time Line 6.0 are accompanied by a substantially revised interface. The previous release's 32 tools and toolbar are gone, replaced by a floating tool palette whose contents are customizable (but whose size and shape, unfortunately, are not). The box-shaped palette blocks enough of the main viewing window to be a nuisance no matter where you put it.

When you start a project, the first screen you will see is Time Line's OverView – a table of contents for projects, resources, calendars, tasks, and tools. Its six sections – Projects, Calendars, Resource Views, Layouts, Conditions, and Custom Columns – let you directly access project information and customize your project environment. OverView is a supervisor's tool: It works best when you need to keep tabs on extremely large or interrelated projects. Its collapsible outline format (reminiscent of Symantec's old GrandView PIM) lets you drop down quickly through several levels and examine a project in any degree of detail.

Note that Time Line does not switch out views of charts and spreadsheets from a single window; instead, it automatically opens multiple windows, one for each view you request. PERT charts, Gantt charts, task-sorted spreadsheets, resource histograms – they are all linked, and the multiple views work great when seen at high resolution.

But when you are running Windows on an 800x600 or 640x480 display, Time Line's tiled windows become illegible because of inadequate viewing space. Cascading the windows is not a solution – you spend more time selecting the view you need than working with resources and tasks. You can close any individual view, of course, but must do so manually. And when you open an existing database, Time Line loads and opens all its views, too – a tedious time- and system-resource-consuming procedure.

These interface changes show Symantec's readiness to find newer, more comprehensive methods of accessing project management information. However, they fail in one crucial respect: They do not give you enough choice. You can not select the old toolbar over the new tool palette, or choose a single viewing window and switch out different views by clicking a button. Nor can you avoid the Overview screen – it is always generated with a project, and closing it closes the database. Time Line 6.0 tells you what is good for you, and requires that you accept its way of doing things.

This approach works well if you have a 17-inch or larger monitor with 1,024x768 or higher resolution; such a configuration lets you see Time Line's resource histogram, period/cumulative cost graph, Gantt spreadsheet/chart, and OverView onscreen at the same time, giving you a comprehensive view of project structure, resource workloads, and cash flow over time. Without such an expansive display and video driver, however, Time Line 6.0 pushes many software features into a small hardware box.

Conclusions

Any of these four programs can satisfy the project management needs of the small business consultant, unless those needs demand one of the ultra high-end packages. In the end, the best program will depend on the personal preferences of the small business consultant. The discussion provided here is merely intended to provide the consultant with data to make an informed decision.

References and Recommended Sources

Foley, James, William May, James Keane, Shiv Hatti, Katherine Wilson, 1996. *Comparison of Mid-Level Project Management Software Applications.* Unpublished Classroom Project.

Frame, Davidson J. 1990. *Managing Projects in Organizations.* Oxford: Jossey-Bass Publishers.

Lewis, James P. 1991. *Project Planning, Scheduling & Control.* Chicago: Probus Publishing Co.

Reschke, H. & H. Schelle. 1990. *Dimensions of Project Management.* Berlin: Springer-Verlag.

The, Lee. April 1996. IS-Friendly Project Management, *Datamation*, 79 - 81.

When Time is Money. Winter 1997. *Fortune*, 122 - 124.

Appendix 2

Small Group Facilitation

This appendix is prepared to help the small business consultant facilitate small group sessions in business, government, or non-profit organizations. We envision work with groups of 5 to 19 people, most frequently natural work groups; that is, people from the same business, working on organizational changes. Four perspectives on small group dynamics are summarized in this appendix:

- Psychodynamic Perspective
- Social Psychological: Group Cohesion & Socialization
- Social Psychological: Influence
- Social Psychological: Decision Making

The Consultant as Facilitator

For each of the four perspectives discussed in this appendix, the consultant would need to do the following as a facilitator of these groups:

- Insure that meetings are efficient; that values, goals, conflicts, problems, and minority positions are available for group action.
- Insure that communications are effective, factual and relevant.
- Insure that the group establishes effective group norms and behavioral guidelines.
- Create processes for the group to clarify values and goals, to anticipate problems, and to develop plans.
- Create group interactions that balance creativity and conclusions, and balance clarity and passion.

In addition, the facilitator should work within the *principle of autonomy*, honoring the free will and responsibility of each participant, where social interaction is free from coercion (Thayer, 1973).

Psychodynamic Perspective: Assumptions And Theoretical Basis

The psychodynamic perspective assumes that group dynamics are heavily influenced by the unconscious psychological dynamics of individual members in the group. A psychological dynamic may be shared among group members or unique to an individual member. Our analysis deals with the psychodynamics that are more commonly shared and are expected to arise in small groups. If we did not use commonly occurring dynamics, we would have to psychoanalyze each group member to use the insights available from this perspective. Luckily, this is not necessary.

Basic premises and assumptions of this perspective include:

- A fear of acknowledging motivations is a major influence in small group interactions.
- Individual group members are, to varying degrees, unaware of the effect that their defenses against acknowledging this fear have on their behavior.
- Groups are influenced by factors completely external to group interactions, such as personality or developmental issues, past traumas, or universal existential issues faced by all men and women, such as the fear of abandonment, and anxiety over the human condition.
- Individuals are defensive; that is, they rationalize behavior in a way that keeps the drives that they fear from becoming clear to them or to others in the group. They work hard at keeping the secrets hidden.

The value of this perspective is its focus on the unconscious psychological factors that might influence group dynamics. One must look for the hidden motivations and fears to understand group dynamics from this perspective. Members of groups only partially accept and acknowledge the psychological "baggage" that they bring to the group. They distort reality to keep their dark secrets hidden. Group members defend their attitudes and behaviors, rather than acknowledge the darker, chaotic side of anxiety, abandonment, and the angst of the human condition.

Observables

Observables are behaviors or characteristics of a small group that are indicators of potential group problems.

Inability to Express Dissent: Dummy Up.   Inability of members of small groups to openly express dissent, feelings, or other reservations is an observable for this type of group. This leads to a poor evaluation of alternatives. The group will "dummy up." This expression captures what is going on. It is the repression and suppression of intellectual and emotional differences in small groups. Members will even make errors in perception in order to avoid disagreement with the majority. A symptom of "dummying up" is the absence of discussion and alternative generation.

Creating Scapegoats or Heroes.   We create scapegoats to carry our blame, our guilt, and our shame. The dissenter role (scapegoats or heroes) functions as a container for envy, competition, and critical evaluation. There are two types of dissenters; positive or negative. Creating a scapegoat increases mindlessness. The group's "dis-ease" is placed on the scapegoat and all other group members can relax. Creating a positive dissenter role can move the group to new and innovative solutions. However, positive "scapegoating" is neither a necessary or sufficient condition for creativity. A facilitator must look for the habitual dissenter - positive or negative - to see if the group is avoiding an issue or problem by creating a scapegoat.

Pigeon Holing and Role Stereotyping. When task assignments are made on the basis of stereotypes (e.g., based on gender), relevant criteria such as skill, knowledge, interest, or resource availability are ignored. "Collective projective identification" is occurring, that is, members are "pigeon holed" and the group suffers.

Diagnostic Questions

Table A2-1 provides a list of questions to diagnose whether the group is experiencing trouble with these dynamics.

Table A2-1: Diagnostic Questions - Psychodynamic Perspective

> **To be asked of the group or to be observed by the consultant:**
>
> *1. Is one member of the group always the scapegoat?*
> "Scapegoating" tends to allow the group to avoid issues and reduce performance and growth. Responsibility for problems is avoided by the group members. Allowing a dissenter, a hero, to carry the responsible for a favored idea may be positive for achieving group goals. However, it may also limit the development and growth of other group members if the behavior is recurring over long periods of time.
>
> *2. Are emotions expressed freely in the group?*
> A positive response indicates that each member of the group is aware of his own apparent intellectual and emotional uniqueness and is willing to accept the unique feelings that other members experience. It also tends to indicate a willingness to learn from the emotional experiences of others.
>
> *3. Are members impatient when others express emotions?*
> Impatience indicates that emotions are not accepted as a valuable source of information. The fact that members are allowed time to express feelings, but this expression is met with some impatience indicates some ambivalence for the value of the emotional data to the group. This is common in a scientifically and economically oriented society in which hard facts and hard currency tend to be the standard of value.

4.   Is there evidence of repressed topics or feelings that are relevant to the task or relationship?
The use of shared fantasy as common ground for group members is not in itself positive or negative. One must decide if the group members are engaging in fantasy in a way that is contributing to or detracting from achieving group goals and individual growth.

5.   Do the group members share enough common experience for the potential of empathy to exist?
One of the problems encountered in groups that are thrown together to solve a problem is that they do not have enough common experience to feel empathy for each other. One solution is to remind members that and to acknowledge that we all share the common experience of being human. Stories about children are often used in this way. If the members seem unable to relate to one another take time out to develop shared experiences.

6. Do group members see the group leader as unavailable, indifferent, or aloof?
The fear of abandonment is a common fear. A group leader who is unavailable, indifferent, or aloof triggers the fear of abandonment among group members. It does not matter that the fear is unjustified or that the leader's behavior does not influence the group's ability to accomplish its task. The fear resides in the group members and is activated by the perceived behavior of the leader.

7. Do members speak of the leader in exaggerated terms?
When group members attribute exaggerated characteristics to the leader; it is a sign that the fear of abandonment is beginning to take hold of the group. Members will complain that the leader is unavailable, does not participate with them, does not offer guidance. In many ways the leader becomes a silent, disinterested, remote figure. Members find that their unconscious anxiety about the human existential condition has surfaced. They want some relief from anxiety and initiate discussion to rid them of the group leader. These behaviors have little to do with the achievement of group goals.

8. Do members speak of wanting to get rid of the leader in abstract or graphic terms?
The frustration over the struggle of dependence and independence, as well as feelings of anxiety due to a sense of abandonment lead members to a revolt against the leader. One should make sure that the revolt is one to change specific behaviors and make specific improvement in the behaviors of group leaders. One should be suspicious of a group's desire to rid itself of the leader, unless there is strong evidence of behavior that is inept. On occasion removing the leader is appropriate. But most often the desire to remove the leader is due to the frustration of the fans. Ask any baseball or football coach.

9. Is stereotyping obvious in task or role assignments?
While it is illegal to discriminate on the basis of sex, age, race, etc. legislation of ethics only forces compliance at some minimum level. We depend upon enlightenment to move above this floor. In the relative privacy of small groups, stereotyping of behavior expectations and other forms of discrimination may be obscured and can undermine the potential and contributions of members (not to mention their human dignity).

10. Are there pressures for certain members to behave according to a set of expectations or are members free to exhibit a range of behaviors?
One frequently finds gender role stereotyping in the assignment of tasks. More insidiously there are expectations about speech patterns and demeanor that are projected on to group members. Deviations from these prescribed behaviors are meet with criticism and pressure to conform to expectations.

> **11. Does the group seem to be occupied by concerns that do not relate to the group interaction?**
> Outside influences on group interaction may appear to be more relevant to member behavior than group interaction. The psychodynamics of each member created outside the group are present with each member and result in interactions that have little to do with the group task. A facilitator should make the group members aware of the individual unconscious dynamics that are prevalent, so that their effect on group productivity may be reduced.

Social Psychological Perspective: Group Cohesion and Socialization

The social psychological perspective assumes that the social context is an important determinant of individual behavior in small groups. This perspective assumes that the group has an identity that is more than the sum of the individual members. In this perspective there is a *groupness* that is "real." The social psychological perspective is quite different from the psychodynamic perspective in that the former tends to explain individual action in terms of conscious cognitive processes, rather than unconscious drives, impulses and fears. It assumes that group members are largely successful in their efforts to act "rationally." These conscious mental processes, such as attitudes, attributions, and beliefs, help explain group dynamics.

In the social psychological perspective, since the group is a real entity and the whole is more than the sum of its parts, the group has characteristics that are different from the members' characteristics. Group membership is seen as having a benefit that members evaluate against the cost of belonging. This cost/benefit analysis of group belonging by members is unique to this perspective.

The assumptions described here apply to all of the variations of the social psychological perspective. These assumptions will not be repeated for each variation.

Assumptions and Theoretical Basis

There are a number of ways to approach the issue of group cohesion and the socialization of members. First, one might look at the characteristics of groups or the characteristics of individual members. One would analyze such things as the individual member's motives or needs; the incentive properties of the group, such as goals, type of interdependence, atmosphere, size, structure, etc.; what members expect from belonging to a group; and the comparison that members make about belonging to one group versus another.

A second view is to look at the stage of development in group membership. Members go through transitional stages of membership beginning with entry, then acceptance, divergence, and exit. This view suggests that member characteristics influence the ease with which a member assimilates into a group. Ease of assimilation means that the members would move through the transition stages easily.

The third point of view analyzes group cohesion and socialization from the perspective of group and individual goals. More convergence between individual and group goals will lead to higher group cohesion. Three types of goals are discussed: utilitarian goals, knowledge goals, and identity goals. *Utilitarian goals* are the tangible outcome goals of a group. *Knowledge goals* have to do with the fact that people depend on each other for verification about how the world works. Individuals corroborate each others knowledge. *Identity goals* relate to individual and group needs for a positive social identity or for "bragging rights." Each of these goals provide a different basis for interdependence among group members, and therefore they provide a basis for group cohesion.

With this as background, we define group cohesion and socialization as follows. *Group cohesion* "refers to the degree to which the members of the group desire to remain in the group... Members of a highly cohesive group...are more concerned with their membership, more strongly motivated to contribute to the group's welfare, to advance its objectives, and to participate..." (Cartwright, 1968, p 91). Thus, group cohesion is an important determinant of member behavior and group dynamics. *Socialization* addresses how individuals are assimilated into full-fledged group membership. A facilitator, aware of the determinants and consequences of group cohesion and member socialization, will be better prepared to facilitate groups that may suffer from insufficient "togetherness," or that do not easily accept new member contributions to group success.

As a consultant, one can improve a group's capacity to assimilate new members by raising member's awareness of group dynamics, and group recruitment skills. The group can learn socialization skills. The consultant may promote these skills by assigning mentors or patrons for new members.

Observables

Level of Participation, Turnover, and Absenteeism. In groups with low cohesiveness, little motivation exists to contribute to the group's welfare, to advance group objectives, or to participate in group activities. Motivation cannot be directly observed but behavioral acts that demonstrate indifference to the group can be observed. Little participation, high turnover, and high absenteeism are consequences of low cohesion. Unmotivated members do not care about group objectives or outcomes. They are absent from group activities. The ultimate failure to participate is to quit the group. High turnover in membership is a symptom of low group cohesiveness.

On occasion, one will encounter a group that is highly cohesive. Members in the group can become so comfortable with each other that they will not leave at almost any cost. This type of group cohesion can lead to apathy, and an inappropriate level of comfort with just belonging to the group. No turnover in a long-standing group might mean no new ideas. One could test the extent to which a group is stuck in this way by proposing changes in membership, objectives, agenda, etc. The response will indicate the amount of discomfort the group will experience with the changes suggested.

Vitality of Group. This observable is similar to participation, but it applies to overall group activity rather than the observation of individual members. If the group has a consistently low energy level and there seems to be little enthusiasm in the group, then this may be a sign of low cohesion. If group cohesion is high, willingness to participate and enthusiasm in support of group goals will be evidenced. Since groups with high cohesiveness do not expend energy on conflicts, they can direct their energy to completing the group task. A sign of a highly cohesive group is the willingness and flexibility that members demonstrate in tackling a group problem.

The Existence of Cliques. Cliques or subgroups within a group signal low cohesiveness and may be evidenced more by interactions outside formal group meetings. These would not be easily observed by a consultant who is not looking for evidence of low cohesiveness. Ironically, high cohesiveness may also make new member assimilation difficult. Long-term members may be so comfortable with each other that they do not want "new blood".

Goal Congruence. When members do not know what the group's goals are, or are not aligned to group goals, cohesion may be low. Low cohesiveness in a group will lead to a clash of individual and group goals. High cohesiveness will result in coherent group objectives and goals.

Lack of Diversity. A potential problem of highly cohesive groups is the unwillingness or inability to deal with diversity. This is especially true if much of the group's cohesiveness is due to similarity of ideas, socioeconomic position, ideology or experience. High cohesiveness may result in answers that are reached quickly, without adequate consideration of alternatives. One way to have an efficient group is to have a group whose members not only do not disagree, but who are not very different from one another. Diversity of ideas is a necessary condition for new and creative insights. A highly cohesive group may limit creativity by restricting confrontation and avoiding a competition of ideas.

Diagnostic Questions

Table A2-2 provides a list of questions to diagnose whether the group is experiencing trouble with these dynamics.

Table A2-2: Diagnostic Questions - Group Cohesion and Socialization

To be asked of the group or to be observed by the consultant:
1) Is there a high level of turnover in group membership? High turnover is an indication of low group cohesiveness. If the group is operating under conditions that require frequent change in group membership, then high turnover could cause low

group cohesiveness. Whether turnover is a cause or effect of low cohesiveness, a facilitator would need to address the situation. The exact adjustment to be made will depend upon the specifics of the situation.

2. Is the group aging and experiencing no turnover? Are group meetings characterized as lethargic?

While it is easy to imagine the problems associated with high turnover in a group, very often the opposite situation could be a problem. A group which has high cohesiveness and has not introduced new members could become "stale" in their perspectives and in their ability to suggest fresh insights or solutions. Groups tend to age, and may lose vitality and passion for their work (N.B. group aging is neither a necessary or sufficient condition for a low levels of creativity, vitality, or productivity). However, if a group exhibited low energy behaviors, then it would be appropriate for a facilitator to examine the extent to which complacency might be ended by the introduction of new members.

3. Do members refuse to participate in the work of the group when asked to volunteer for assignments?

When group cohesiveness is low, the willingness to advance the group's goals and interests are lower. Members will not be inclined to participate in the work of the group. The specific context in which this behavior occurs must be examined by the facilitator. Failure to participate may be due to a variety of causes, such as personal problems, time limitations, etc.. One should also look for evidence that would suggest that the failure to participate is symptomatic of low cohesiveness in a group.

4. Are members constantly gossiping and speaking negatively about one another?

Constant gossiping and negative evaluations of members by members is indicative of low cohesion. This behavior will also reduce cohesion by making either or both the person gossiping and the subject of gossip less attractive in the eyes of other members. One should request or suggest a group norm that disallows chronic and non-factual evaluation of one another.

5. Do members evaluate membership in the group less favorably than membership in some other group?

If members of group A evaluate membership in group B as more attractive, then it is likely that the desire to be in group A will be reduced. Group cohesion will also be reduced. A facilitator can use the information on which the comparison is based as a way of improving the group performance and possibly forestall a drop in group cohesion.

6. Do members express high levels of anxiety, or low levels of self esteem in talking about their membership in the group?

When there is low group cohesiveness, group members express anxiety and feelings of low self esteem when talking about their membership in the group. These feelings tend to lead to lower levels of participation, lower productivity, and desire to leave the group. High group cohesiveness would promote a sense of security in belonging to the group. High group cohesiveness would tend to increase member support of group activities and goals. While feelings of anxiety, low self esteem, and other negative emotions may be caused by other factors, group cohesiveness is also a potential cause.

7. Do members associate with each other freely? Do members form cliques and limit interaction only to these subgroups within the group?

In groups with high cohesion, members freely associate with each other. Cliques or factions do not tend to develop in highly cohesive groups. Limited interaction will tend to limit the amount of information and skill sharing in a group. It also limits cooperation in accomplishing group objectives. A facilitator could encourage more cohesion

8. *Do members know the group's goals? Can they articulate the group's purpose?*
Members of highly cohesive groups will be able to articulate group goals consistently with each other. There will be a shared sense of purpose that is known and accepted by each member. Members of groups with low cohesion are more likely to express confusion about group goals, or to differ in the articulation of group goals and objectives. A facilitator may enhance group cohesiveness by having the group develop common goals and objectives that are valued by members. If members value group goals, they will tend to evaluate more highly their membership in the group.

9. *Where is the "gate" for entry and exit from the group? Who is the gatekeeper?*
The dynamics of entry and exit from the group are important to a sense of belonging or cohesion. If the gate is always open and members enter and leave with little acknowledgment or ritual, then group cohesiveness is low. If the gate on group membership is closed tightly and forever, then entry and exit is impossible. A closed gate may increase group cohesiveness, but it can be dangerous to group effectiveness or survival (a good example of this is the Shaker religion).

10. *Is the group aware of its stage of development? Does the group take time to discuss its status as a group?*
Groups develop through different stages. Transition points mark the movement from one stage to the next. The stages are: investigation, socialization, maintenance, re-socialization, and remembrance. In the investigation stage members are found and recruited. A transition point called entry marks the passage from the investigation to the socialization stage. In the socialization stage members are assimilated into the group and accommodate each other. The second transition point is acceptance which marks the end of socialization and the beginning of the maintenance stage. Role negotiation occurs in the maintenance stage. When members diverge, the third transition point, they move from the maintenance stage to the re-socialization stage in which new assimilation and/or accommodations are made. The final transition point is exit from the group, which leads to the remembrance stage during which tradition is developed and members reflect on their experiences.

Awareness of the stage of development of a group will allow a consultant to attenuate the group to the social or relational aspects of that stage, and thereby legitimize or "give the group permission" to take time to progress through that stage. Often groups believe that they must evaluate and choose solutions to problems and therefore do not acknowledge the need for social development.

11) *Is the group so socially cohesive that members refuse to tackle issues that threaten group cohesiveness?*
Group members can become so comfortable with each other that they will not take on tasks or confront each other if there is any risk to the cohesiveness of the group. This would be a highly cohesive group, but not a well functioning group. If members place too high a value on cohesiveness, they threaten the group's existence by not attending to its creativity and its productivity.

Social Psychological Perspective: Influence

The assumptions and theoretical basis summarized for the social psychological perspective also apply to the discussion of influence. Influence, as an aspect of group dynamics, assumes that the interaction of individuals in a group setting causes change in the individual's opinion, attitude, beliefs or positions. As a consultant, it is useful to have at least a working knowledge of the various theories and frameworks in order to understand the determinants, processes, and consequences of influence in small groups.

The major factors that affect how influence occurs in small groups are:

- the type of influence, that is, normative or informational; proactive, inertial, or counteractive; or other types of influence such as reward, coercion, expert, referent, legitimate, information;
- the nature of the task;
- the decision rule used, such as unanimity or majority rule;
- the difference between public congruence and private congruence;
- the types of conformity, and the difference between conformity and innovation and the effect of size of majorities and minorities on conformity.

This perspective has numerous frameworks, and provides a rich dimensionalization of influence in small groups.

Types of Influence

There are many classification schemes for the construct of influence. Influence may be thought of in majority and minority terms. Majority influence results in conformity to the majority position. Minority influence results in innovation in the sense of a shift away from the majority opinion to the minority position.

Another useful distinction is made between normative and informational influence. Normative influence is sharing one's preference or value position with another, and as a result of this interaction, there is a change in the individual's preferences or value position. Informational influence is the use of facts, rationale, and argument to change a person's decision or ideas about a subject. We address the importance of this distinction later.

Other types of influence are proactive, inertial, and counteractive. This classification addresses the extent to which the influence causes a group to move toward a goal (proactive); to remain in its current status, either moving toward goals or being stuck (inertial); or to move farther away from its goals (counteractive).

Another classification scheme describes the bases or mechanisms of influence, such as influencing through reward, coercion, expertise, referent (the attractiveness of association with a group or individual), legitimate (based on authority), and informational bases (Levine and Russo, 1987, p 21).

Type of task. If the group is working on a *judgment task*, that is, a decision of preference, a value position, or an issue of ethics or morality, then attempts to influence others by using facts and arguments (i.e., informational influence) will frequently fail. If a group is working on a task that has a "correct" answer that can be determined by the application of good research, an *intellective task*, then informational influence works best. The use of facts, logic, and argument to resolve preferences and values, often fails to influence people who are dealing with normative questions or issues that have a strong emotional component. It is often better to allow a dialogue that will bring forth the sense, sensibility, and intuition of the group members, than to argue facts and figures logically. If the tool does not fit the task, then the job is more difficult or even impossible. That is not to say that all facts, logic, and argument be excluded from a discussion of normative issues. It is to say, however, that judgment tasks will ultimately be decided on values rather than data and logic. Matching type of influence and task will reduce the miscommunication and frustration in group interactions.

Decision Rules. The effect that influence attempts have on group members, is conditioned by the type of decision rule used by the group. For example, if a group uses a majority decision rule while completing a judgment task, there is a tendency for members to feel more discontent. If a group uses a unanimity decision rule when working on a judgment task, then member satisfaction is greater. There tends to be less member frustration when intellective tasks are addressed using a majority rule. A facilitator might find that a group is less effective than it could be if the combination of the types of influence, task, and decision rule are mismatched (Kaplan, 1987).

Types Of Conformity. It is important to understand the difference between public and private conformity. Compliance is public agreement, but private disagreement. Acceptance is public and private agreement or congruence. It is possible to have an individual express public congruence with the majority position, but privately disagree. Conformity is a shift in position of a minority member to the majority position. Innovation, technically speaking, is a majority member's shift to the minority position. Conformity and innovation are affected by type of influence.

Observables

Talking Past One Another. Talking past one another is an indication that members are not open to mutual influence. Establishing rules for active listening, dialogue, or simple norms of exchanging information and points of view will be useful for groups that do not listen to one another.

Unwillingness or Inability to Express Dissent. Another behavior indicative of the unwillingness to influence is the failure of group members to express their opinion or provide factual input to the group discussion. This behavior could be in response to the status differences among members; to the perceived risks from sources outside the group; to perceived or real power differences; or to different hierarchical positions of members. More egalitarian group norms reduce the probability that members will withhold their participation in the group discussion.

Diagnostic Questions

Table A2-3, on the following page, provides a list of questions to diagnose whether the group is experiencing trouble with these dynamics.

Table A2-3: Diagnostic Questions - Influence

To be asked of the group or to be observed by the facilitator:

1) Is the group clear on the type of problem it has to solve?
Group tasks can be categorized as normative and intellective tasks. Intellective tasks have a right answer that can be ascertained by facts, logic, and an analysis of the evidence. It is useful for the group to know clearly how progress toward normative and interceptive tasks is differentially affected by influence strategy, decision rules, group size, etc.

2. Are group members aware of the different types of influence and when to apply them?
Normative influence works best with normative tasks. Informational influence works best with intellective tasks. A mismatch of influence strategy and type of task can cause problems for group interaction. Influence based on expertise, experience would be more effective on intellective tasks. Referent and legitimate influence works best with normative tasks.

3) Are there certain members prone to use specific types of influence regardless of the group task?
Group members may use certain influence styles out of habit. The group's chance of success is reduced when members do not have the flexibility to adapt influence behaviors that are appropriate for different tasks, decision rules, or group characteristics.

4) Do authority relationships exist between members? What are they?
One group member in a position of authority can create pluralistic ignorance among group members. Pluralistic ignorance is evidenced by group member's silence. It arises when members are concerned that expressed opinions will threaten their personal well being and status in the group or organization. As a facilitator, one way to deal with the issue is to coach group members on how to disagree with an authority figure in non-threatening ways. There may be situations when disagreeing with a person in authority in a non-threatening manner is an oxymoron. Caution is mandatory in such situations.

5. How are group members who hold minority opinions treated by the group?
Group members holding a minority position have the difficult task of convincing those in the majority to accept what is a less "popular" position. This is especially difficult with normative tasks. Much of the confidence in a particular position is based on the confirmation that one receives from others. A minority member is well advised to avoid a defensive response to influence attempts by the majority, and to use influence attempts that are appropriate for the task at hand. For example, normative tasks are best influenced by arguments of preference and value. Intellective tasks, those with a knowable correct answer, are best argued using facts and logic.

6. *Do the members of the group have equal status*?
Status has an effect on group interaction that is similar to authority. It tends to create deference. If the most competent arguments and the best alternatives are not presented by the person of status or authority, and if status or authority prevail, then the group outcomes will suffer.

7. *Do members attempt to influence the group outcomes by disruptive behavior?*
There are times when disruptive behavior is used to influence group outcomes. This is a form of influence that is brutish and difficult. The best strategy is to avoid defensive reaction. One must find out why reasoned discussion has been abandoned. If possible, remove the reason for the disruptive behavior by listening.

8. *Do group members share the same goals and objectives?*
When group members share the same goals, then it is less likely that public conformity will mask private dissent. Influence attempts will tend to be constructive. Goal congruence provides a basis of agreement and cooperation. Goal congruence allows members to focus on their common interests.

9. *Do members really change their position or are they simply publicly complying?*
This perspective makes an important distinction between public compliance and private acceptance. Members acquiesce to the majority opinion to avoid an unpleasant confrontation. They may privately retain a strong opposition to that position. This discrepancy between publicly expressed and privately held viewpoints can be very harmful to a group. Influence attempts that are coercive are more likely to result in this public - private split. For example, if members are threatened by economic harm or lower status; are rewarded to take on a point of view; or anticipate the use of authority or power, then it is possible for members to have different public and private positions. A consultant should encourage the proper use of authority and power.

Social Psychological Perspective: Decision Making

Decision making, an aspect of the social psychological perspective, assumes that decision rules and decision process affect the quality of group decisions. We will summarize the effect of decision rules on decision making and decision making errors.

Decision Rules

Decision rules influence group interaction and have psychological consequences that affect the quality of decision making. The "strictness" of the decision rule and the distribution of power are the two most important features of decision rules. Strictness is the degree of difficulty that the decision rule imposes on members' decision making. Distribution of power relates to the ability to influence a decision.

The most common decision rules are unanimity, majority rule, and dictatorship. Decision rules affect how people behave, how they think, and how they feel, including:

- a group's ability to reach a decision;
- the number of alternatives considered;

- the quality of the decision;
- member satisfaction;
- the content of the group discussion;
- perceptions of fairness;
- perceptions of the group by outsiders;
- the time spent on reaching a decision.

Table A2-4 summarizes the effect of decision rules on group dynamics and decision making.

Table A2-4: Effect of Decision Rules on Group Dynamics

Group Dynamics	Decision Rule Used by Group		
	Unanimity	Majority Rule	Dictatorship
Nature of Decision	• All members agree • The most strict • Increases failure to reach a decision • More compromise • Creates movement toward extremes	• 50% plus 1 rules • Less strict than unanimity • Less failure to reach a decision than with unanimity • Compromise less	• One person decision; least strict decision rule • No interaction needed to decide • No compromise needed
Preferences of members	• Tends to align preferences	• Not as close to member preferences	• Member preference can be made irrelevant
Member Satisfaction with Decision	• Greater satisfaction due to greater agreement, especially on decision requiring judgments	• Members are less satisfied; especially for decision requiring judgment	• Member satisfaction will be low if the outcome is not representative of member preferences
Duration & Content of Discussion	• Discussion takes longer • More thorough & adequate discussion	• Discussion is less comprehensive than unanimity; not all members must be considered	• Discussion is not necessary and depending upon leadership style will center upon preferences of leader
Perceptions of Discussion	• Uncomfortable, difficult, conflict laden,	• Easier, more enjoyable discussion	• Varies, depending on leadership style
Member Perceptions of Fairness	• More perceived fairness since decisions are more representative and there is more agreement	• More often considered unfair because decision is often less representative	• Perception of fairness if outcomes are representativeness of member positions
Member attraction to one another	• Members are more attracted to one another due to more agreement	• Less attractiveness among members due to need for less agreement	• Attractiveness among members is difficult to predict
Group Attribution Error*	• More representative of member preferences, less room for attribution error	• Outcomes are often less representative, thus there is more room for attribution error	• Most room for the wrong assumptions about member positions

* Group Attribution Error, that is, outsiders belief that group outcomes reflect member preferences

Decision Making Errors

Decision making errors arise from three sources. The first source is the recognition or assessment of the problem or decision. This problem is often due to the group's failure to recognize that the problem exists at all (i.e., denial). Groups also make errors in their diagnosis of the cause of the problem. For example, sales are falling and the group decides to fire a sales person. It turns out that the quality of the product has dropped due to equipment problems. Firing the sales person did not eliminate the root cause.

A second source of group error is failure to establish specific goals, or establishing unnecessary goals. If goals are general or abstract, then there is room to reinterpret (or misinterpret) the goal. Room for interpretation means that there is room for change and disagreement. A third source of error is the group's failure to accurately assess the positive and negative consequences of the alternatives considered.

Groups increase the possibility of error if, by their interactions, they establish a flawed information base, or if they encourage faulty reasoning. For example, faulty reasoning can occur due to "escalating commitment" to a course of action. Pressure to agree encourages members to use data to support prior preferences.

Groupthink   Groupthink is "a mode of thinking that people engage in when they are deeply involved in a cohesive group, when the members' striving for unanimity override their motivation to realistically appraise alternative courses of action" (Janis, 1972, p 8). Two well known disasters that are attributed to groupthink are the Challenger explosion and the Bay of Pigs Invasion. The conditions that make a group vulnerable to groupthink are high cohesiveness, expressed leadership preferences, and a group that is insulated from expert advice. The symptoms of groupthink are: a sense of invulnerability; the tendency of the group to rationalize away warnings or negative data; stereotypical views of others; pressure to agree, especially if done by making emotional appeals; the illusion that everyone agrees without checking; and mindguarding, that is, keeping adverse information away from the group.

There are a few decision making techniques that may help reduce the occurrence of groupthink:

- Encourage the generation and consideration of many alternative solutions, including a willingness to re-examine alternatives that have been dismissed. The situation or information may change, thus making a previously discarded option more attractive;
- Use outside expert advice to expand the information base and enhance alternative generation;

- Promote a willingness to discuss and accept negative information about a preferred or previously established position;
- The group might generate contingency plans. This draws attention to the positive and negative consequences of the group's decision.

Observables

There are many "observables" provided in Table A2-4 and the brief discussion of groupthink. Here are a few additional observables of consequence:

Oppression of the Minority   The use of majority rule may lead to suppression of the minority position. This pattern is easily seen when majority rule is evoked spontaneously, in the midst of conflict, without positive consideration to the task, the group, the minority, or the adverse consequences on the minority interest. Another indication of the misuse of majority rule is the lack of an appeal procedure.

Cohesion Over Correction   A highly cohesive group may value cohesion more than correcting perceptions, judgments, or opinions. Cohesive groups might maintain an inaccurate position rather than "rock the boat". Scapegoating, hastily discounting dissenting positions, or marginalizing the worth of a member or a member's position are signs of a group that values cohesion over the quality of performance.

Process Wallow   Process wallow is the tendency of some groups to avoid making progress against an objective by re-hashing issues. Process wallow is more likely to occur when decision rules are strict. Process wallow can be one way that cohesive groups avoid the unpleasant social consequences of confrontation. This is especially true if group members conclude that delay or avoidance does not have catastrophic consequences.

Answers Before the Question   Groups will frequently enter an interaction with a list of possible solutions to a problem that has not been clearly identified nor articulated. Groups that are pressed for time seem to believe that time is saved by proposing solutions quickly, that is, "by getting down to solving the problem." Clear solutions to the wrong problem obviously put performance at risk.

Facts Support Fiction   Group members may use facts to support their prior position. This may even extend to selective perception and the omission of relevant information. These problems of information processing on the individual level can be exaggerated at the group level by what can be an almost contagious excitement over a possible solution, even when the solution is premature or inappropriate. Group interaction can reinforce and magnify individual error.

Diagnostic Questions

Table A2-5 provides a list of questions to diagnose whether the group is experiencing trouble with these dynamics.

<u>Table A2-5:</u> Diagnostic Questions - Decision Making

To be asked of the group or to be observed by the consultant:

1. Has the group consciously selected the decision rule?
Groups may begin problem solving without explicitly evaluating the decision rule they are going to use. Research shows that a mismatch between the type of task and the decision rule used can lead to lower quality decisions and less member satisfaction. For example, the unanimity decision rule is more likely to enhance group performance when the group must make a value judgment or establish a preference based on their opinion and beliefs.

2. Does the process allow enough time to adequately identify and clearly articulate the problem?
Groups will frequently feel time pressure and begin solving the problem before it is clear. When this happens members may be working on different tasks. As the group process continues, the view that each member has of the task changes. After discussion, the task can become quite different, and this change may become a problem to group performance and to the relationships among members.

3. Are the members sufficiently confident in their relationship to allow conflict?
Unanimity decision rules will at times strain the relationships among members. Members become impatient with the "time wasted on conflicts." Instead of seeing conflict and confrontation as a process of working out differences of opinion, it is seen as a threat to social cohesion. Members must be confident in their relationship with each other to be willing to confront each other.

4. How is new information, contradictory to the prevalent group position, received?
If a group has established a majority position, new information may be excluded because the group does not want to "lose ground." Reconsidering a decision in the face of new information may be thought of as being redundant work and a waste of time. Pressure toward making progress is useful to a group, but one must judge the extent to which such pressure is not allowing valid and important information, options, or insights to be considered. If the new information is not considered, one might raise the topic for discussion and observe reaction. Take care to watch for members who cut off or marginalize members who see value in the new information. The appropriate way to resolve the issue to argue the merits and relevance of the information against the task.

5. How do the majority members treat the minority members?
Majority rule may be used to shut out a minority position in a group. Members know that they don't have to consider every one's point of view, they tend to do only that amount of consideration necessary to reach a majority vote. Important considerations may be omitted from the decision process.

6. Are conditions for groupthink present?
High levels of cohesiveness, group leaders who quickly express their preferences and opinions, and failure to use expert advice are conditions that can lead to groupthink. If a group values the

comfort of mutual reassurance, or ridicules or excludes outsiders based on their beliefs, opinion, or position, then there is a danger that groupthink will influence group performance.

7. Does the organization's culture, or the leader's disposition, strongly influence the decision rules and interaction of the group?

If organization or group leadership pressures strongly influence the decision making process, then the best decision making process may not be used. For example, the president of an organization frequently and publicly states that all key decisions made by the executive team are determined by majority rule. The president is proud of the fact that important policy decisions are made quickly, efficiently, and fairly. It is likely that a group in such an organization will use the majority vote to make decisions. In many situations, this would not be the most useful choice for the group.

8. Is the group working on causes of the problem or symptoms?

Groups that do not work to uncover the true cause or root cause of a problem will not be effective. Such groups might make rapid progress toward a decision, or they might make a large number of decisions quickly. However, they will not solve problems, but at best mask them. For example, an organization fires a marketing person because of eroding market share when the company really needs to improve the quality of its products. The problem may well be the decision not to make product improvements, rather than the marketing manager's performance. If a group must assess the situation, a decision making process that requires careful consideration of all the facts will be most useful in identifying the root cause.

9. Does the group discussion tend toward a presentation of facts, evidence, and logic, or does the group tend to share opinions, insights and preferences?

Group members focused on problem solving can lose sight of, or may be unaware of, the process that best solves the problem. They frequently resort to processes or procedures that have been successful in the past. They might rely on processes and procedures that are commonly used in the organization or society. Common usage may indicate that the process is workable at least in some situations. However. the choice may be based on unfounded superstitious knowledge, rather than evidence that the process actually works. Superstitious behaviors are reasonably common examples of this tendency. The use of majority voting in democratic societies is a habitual decision rule that may not be as effective as the unanimity rule or deferring to an expert.

10. Does one person dominate the group decision making process? What are the consequences?

One person's dominance of the group decision making process effects the group's performance and member relationships. If the dominant person is also the most competent person, then performance can be very good. If the dominant person is not the most competent, then performance will suffer accordingly. The effect on relationships is less predictable. Members can have a wide variety of reactions to a dominant member. For example, they might simply acquiesce, silently resist, or openly confront the dominant member. It is clear that the relationship among members will be affected.

Conclusion

We have presented four perspectives for facilitating small groups. The small business consultant who is adept at group dynamics has a competitive advantage. The four perspectives described, along with the lists of diagnostic questions, have proven helpful to us in our own small business consulting interventions.

References

Cartwright, D. 1968. The Nature of Group Cohesiveness, In D. Cartwright & A. Zander (eds.), *Group Dynamics Research and Theory.* New York: Harper and Row.

Kaplan, M.F. 1987. The Influencing Process in Group Decision-Making, In C. Hendricks (ed.), *Group Processes.* Newbury Park, CA: Sage Publications.

Levine, J.M. and Russo, E.M. 1987. Majority and Minority Influence. In C. Hendricks (ed.), *Group Processes.* Newbury Park, CA: Sage.

Poole, M. S., Group Communication and the Structuring Process. In Cathcart, Samovar, & Henman (eds.), *Small Group Communications: Theory and Practice.* Dubuque, IA: Brown & Benchmark, 85 - 99.

Shaw, M. 1976. The Task Environment, *Group Dynamics: The Psychology of Small Group Behavior.* New York: Mc Graw Hill.

Shoemaker, H. 1991. Self-Construction in a Small Group Setting, *Small Group Research.* 22:3, 339 - 359.

Thayer, Frederick C. 1973. *An End of Hierarchy! An End of Competition: Organizing the Politics and Economics of Survival.* New York: New Viewpoints.

Wood, J., G. Phillips, & D. Pedersen. Understanding the Group as a System. In Cathcart, Samover, and Henman (eds.), *Small Group Communications: Theory and Practice.* Dubuque, IA: Brown & Benchmark, 12 - 24.